Contents

2011 Foreword to the 2008 Edition

It is now Summer 2011, some three years since I spent the summer break after graduation writing down the five hundred thousand words which comprised the book *Freeing Growth: Volume 1*. That book sought to describe the simplest possible understanding of the Universe based on the best available knowledge of our information holographised, least-action thermophysical world, and from that to suggest a series of proposals which ought to substantially increase long term, sustained economic growth.

That unpublished book was, and still is, my best attempt to summarise four years worth of discussions of our little group of undergraduates reading for our degrees at the University of St. Andrews (one of the most ancient and elite universities in the world, and one which has an astonishing concentration of the children of the world's ruling elite, especially from the US, Europe and China). It was a highly personal summary – none of our group would agree with all of it, or even much of it individually, with each having their own set of opinions, though the opinions of each is represented to some degree within the whole. And it suffered from being as complex, intricate and therefore impenetrable to outsiders as four years of conversations between a dozen people must inherently be, so its usefulness outside our group was limited. I am therefore particularly grateful to the staff within the University of St. Andrews, and to those much further afield, who undertook a particularly difficult task of attempting to make sense of it, and for the detailed comments and suggestions that they made.

What follows in this Manifesto is a summary of the main recommendations of that book, incorporating that valuable feedback from our elders, written straight after finishing the main book manuscript in early 2009. At less than sixty pages, it is a manageable though still overwhelming read. It shows that the children of the ruling elite have plenty of ideas on how to fix our planet and our civilisation, and are willing to be as ruthlessly rational as our forefathers were to achieve it. One has to wonder if the baby boomer generation subconsciously suspect this, because they continue to make remarkable efforts to exclude their own progeny from gaining the control, wealth, power and job security necessary to implement the inevitable elimination of most of their old age entitlements and security (according to Gokhale (2009), in 2004 unfunded entitlements by governments alone were 514% of GDP in the US and 434% of GDP in the EU25). **Before** the 2008 recession, of those under the age of twenty-five in Western Europe and the US, some 45% (UK[1]), 51% (US[2]) and 60% (Spain[3]) are economically inactive or in low skilled or temporary employment. Of the 10% (Spain), 22% (US) and 31% (UK) with some job security[4], more than half work more than sixty hours per week (including commuting) (Hewlett & Luce, 2006) which gives barely enough time to spend with children let alone to make use of their resources to enact change, and most of their income is taken by the banks as mortgage interest payments and recycled into growing the pension funds of their parents or the sovereign wealth funds of resource rich developing countries. As the ongoing flat-growth 'recovery' – which the book and this Manifesto predicted – has shown, the first to get fired and stay fired were the youngest. Irrespective of competence, hours worked, or level of qualification.

Of all the proposals made by the book, the chapter on the proposals for old age were the most controversial despite that, in my opinion, they were the least dangerous or severe of any proposed in the book (after all, we do love our parents and we do owe a great – but **proportional** and **realistic** – debt to them!). Indeed, so controversial were they that I was persuaded by those much wiser than I to omit them from the 2009 edition of this Manifesto, and I have felt bad about it ever since. I have therefore restored this missing proposal as proposal 18. Before (some) readers fulminate too hard with rage when reading this restored proposal, I might add that what it proposes is tame compared to some undergraduates who wish to nationalise all private and public pension funds, which in effect simply retroactively abolishes all retirement and grabs

---

[1] Source: http://www.dailymail.co.uk/news/article-1291254/Stop-gap-year-graduates-taking-temp-jobs-beat-unemployment.html, http://www.guardian.co.uk/society/2011/jul/22/youth-employment-rate-lowest

[2] Source: http://bls.gov/news.release/youth.nr0.htm

[3] Source: http://www.aqu.cat/insercio/estudi_2011_graduats_en.html

[4] Sources: http://www.dailymail.co.uk/news/article-1291254/Stop-gap-year-graduates-taking-temp-jobs-beat-unemployment.html, http://www.aqu.cat/insercio/estudi_2011_graduats_en.html., http://www.nationaljurist.com/content/45-employment-rate-how-law-school-employment-numbers-are-inflated

the accumulated wealth. I strongly oppose that solution due to its profound moral hazard, and because I very much doubt that it would wisely spent.

One will no doubt notice that the restored proposal has less of the fire of the original chapters which were deliberately written to imitate the style of *The Communist Manifesto* published by Marx and Engels in 1848, right down to mimicking its opening page. This is quite simply because I am now some three years outside the St. Andrews bubble, and I am no longer inured with the righteous fury made only possible by being surrounded by the radical thought of young minds. In the desire to not lose what I feel is an important part of the original manuscript, I have not modified the text apart from proposal 18 despite that the figures and graphs could do with being updated with the latest data.

Indeed, much as with the rest of most of our age cohort in this recession, all of our group are presently immobilised by either penury or overwork. Johanna had to return to live with her parents in the quiet wilderness of countryside Sweden, and after finishing a postgraduate qualification in music production is currently reflecting on what to do next. Sarah finished a second undergraduate degree in Occupational Therapy and is currently being overworked in two jobs in York. Anneka remains employed in a bar in Edinburgh. Natasja is overworked in Brussels in order to afford a mortgage on a small flat, and with her health slowly failing due to this, she is shortly emigrating to Nigeria where she hopes to be given an opportunity without glass ceilings. Olga went to Warwick for a PhD, and I haven't heard from her since. McKinley moved to London, and has just recently got married – she works part-time in a publishing house. Valentine was being overworked in a property consulting multinational in London, but I haven't heard from her since 2009. Kat and Ingrid I fell out with, and therefore have no idea what has happened to them. Megan, of course, lives with me and my father here in Cork having just completed her second Masters degree and as a fully qualified teacher, faces many years to come of temporary employment with no maternity rights.

When we left St. Andrews, we were all glad to see the back of the place: it is after all where the future ruling elite are trained, and the training is brutal. Our time there was difficult and painful, but certainly stimulating – and no one could say that each and every one of us did not grow immensely. Adjusting to life after St. Andrews has been difficult – where pace was forced relentlessly onto you before, now you have to create your own pace. One looks back with a definite bittersweetness, though wary of positively romanticising the experience as hindsight tends to do.

Common Reactions to this Manifesto

Reactions to these proposals regularly fall into a certain set of categories, and I think it would be useful to the reader if I commented on these.

The first most common reaction is that these proposals are highly elitist. I agree with this reaction. After all, they were generated within one of the most elitist universities in the world – not only does one take having royalty and students driving sports cars around you as normal at St. Andrews, at the time we were there around 15% of all students were Americans on their year abroad from the top Ivy League universities. There was also a good chunk (8% I believe) of students from the rich elites of China and Taiwan, though in my experience only a tiny percentage were willing to interact in any depth with anyone outside their ethnic group, and they certainly weren't willing to discuss any kind of contentious topic even privately. Even among the British students, more than half at St. Andrews were privately educated – around twice the ratio of Cambridge or Oxford. So yes, I would agree that the proposals are indeed highly elitist.

A similar, but semantically different reaction, is that the proposals intend to transfer much recently diversified power from everybody else back to the ruling elites, and as a system of restoring the power and authority of an aristocracy, they therefore represent a step backwards in pluralism. I would also agree with that sentiment in general, but I would caveat it as follows: Firstly, most of the world's present problems have stemmed from allowing people who are too ignorant to know better to do what they want without thinking through the consequences beforehand. The proposals remove all civil liberties from anyone without sufficient current skill qualifications to understand the responsibility which comes with a particular freedom. Secondly, our civilisation is already in decline, and as billions begin to shortly starve to death, the self-destructive hedonism of the masses will either be reigned in through the biosphere eradicating enough of us that civilisation collapses completely, or some form of centrally imposed control (hopefully through something like these proposals rather than a repressive autocracy). If one assumes that some form of authoritarian regime is inevitable (and I feel this preferable than to all going to hell in a hand-basket), then one must ask *what is the best form of authoritarian regime?*

What is proposed in this Manifesto is meritocratic – those who are the best qualified to rule as propelled into those positions. This confers a massive advantage to the existing ruling elites for sure – they have educated their children to the greatest extent, and therefore under the proposed system these children would rapidly occupy the same positions of power as their forefathers. However, the big break with the present (as judged by socioeconomic mobility rate) mostly hereditary system is that all children are given the same basic education until the age of seven, and 5% of the economy is ring fenced to ensure this. After that, the very poorest person is paid to educate themselves just the same as the very richest, but of course each dollar or euro is worth more to the poorer person, so improving oneself is a more likely use of a poorer person's time than a richer person's. What is hard to imagine for those used to contemporary economic thinking is that what is proposed here is an education-driven economy rather than the present resource extraction driven economy, so just imagine a plethora of education instead of the plethora of consumer goods in every home and you're somewhat close to imagining the economy proposed. I don't doubt that intangible wealth such as personal connections won't still confer a huge advantage to the children of the ruling classes, however the point is that the proposed playing field is more meritocratic than either the present field, or that of the middle ages, or indeed at any time hitherto, and is therefore better considered as an improvement to *actual* pluralism rather than theoretical pluralism. What is therefore proposed is indeed a system for restoring power and legitimacy to a ruling elite, but this is a more *meritocratically selected elite*. And, if you think the proposals through, you will see that for most citizens the loss of most liberties would be temporary as they would reacquire them by *earning* the right to exercise them through acquiring the appropriate skill qualifications enabling whichever rights each person values most highly (i.e. effectively one is creating a *market* for individual civil liberties, except that instead of buying liberties with money, one 'rents' liberties through up-to-date skill qualifications). In case you are worried that this system could be interfered with for special candidates, a public key encryption system anonymises all scripts and a peer to peer distributed computer system ensures that grades are partially risked for peer review[5]. Unlike the present pretend 'anonymised' marking system employed by many universities, this system is cryptographically secure. It also, interestingly, makes everyone's grades publicly known to everybody to prevent *ex post* grade modification.

The next most common reaction is that these proposals are heavily centred on the West, and by the West one means the United States and Western Europe to exclusion of all else. The question therefore is raised as to how useful these proposals actually are as the world increasingly globalises and most of the global population is not living in the West. Once again, I agree with the observation: apart from the ethnic block of Chinese and Taiwanese at St.

---

[5] I am actually in the process of writing the software to implement this as part of my Master of Research thesis with the Institute of Education, University of London. The software is called Oxydérkeia and its homepage is at http://www.oxyderkeia.net/.

Andrews, it is almost exclusively made up of Western Europeans and those of the United States, so one would expect the proposals to centre on the world in which we live. I would also agree that the usefulness of these proposals outside the West is limited: the people who live in India, or South America, or China have a different accumulated culture than we do. They therefore have a different package of proposals more suitable to them, or rather more likely a different *presentation* of proposals more suitable to them. I could speculate on what that package might be, but in the end my knowledge of non-Western cultures is necessarily more limited. Put simply, I wouldn't feel myself competent to propose what other cultures ought to do, though I would be more than happy to collaborate in the future with anyone who is more competent than I on these things. In the end, we *are* a globalised civilisation now. We all sink or swim together, and to that end something equally radical needs to be done in non-Western cultures for Western cultures to survive.

Another reaction which commonly comes up is noting how often God is mentioned throughout the text, yet the proposals are very secular. It is often queried why God is in there at all as a result, and therefore that the text would be clearer if all mentions of God were removed. This is an interesting point, and one upon which I can elucidate at considerable length, but this isn't the place to do so. In short, the answer to this is highly complex, but I can assure anyone who cares that God is absolutely essential to these proposals, and that the apparently secular nature of the proposals is in fact a mirage induced in part by our contemporary writing style of English. In particular, when these proposals are computer modelled, you will find that God is held to be the master profit & loss account in the accounting, the source of random noise which drives the iterative models, the spatialisation of structure, and indeed the sum total structure accumulated thus far in the Universe as well as the entropy which drives growth. In other words, God *is* growth, God *is* structure/knowledge, God *is* everything and nothing simultaneously. And, rather heretically for the Abrahamic religions, to perceive i.e. to cognate i.e. to be of matter i.e. to be structured energy generating a gravimetric field is an aspect of God relating to another aspect of God through light, which is of course God. In this, the underlying metaphysics are most definitely Pandeist.

If you are profoundly atheist, or sufficiently religious that this is blasphemy, feel free to replace the word 'God' with the word 'Infiniteness'/'Love'/'Time'. In this sense the proposals are secular: God is taken to be a mathematical concept, so the only things held strongly about the God referred to by this text are those required by the mathematics. Anything other than that is, quite frankly, a personal matter of your own choosing.

So why then choose to map God as a mathematical concept? The answer is twofold: firstly, the last twenty years of making sense of more accurate empirical results across a number of disciplines are converging on what may become the next leap forward in human understanding. In cutting-edge Physics, they keep finding themselves moving beyond the foundation of field theory in a consistent way which has recently been labelled as 'Information Holography'. This holographic (self-mapping, self-transforming) treatment of information has an eerie correspondence with cutting-edge developments in information science and information technology (where it falls under multiple classifications such as 'stream computing', 'semantic networks', 'federated identity' and many others), as well as cutting-edge mathematics (where it tends to fall under the general 'topologies' category, but pops up in all sorts of unexpected niches). As Jacob Bekenstein pointed out in a 2003 Scientific American article (Bekenstein, 2003), our physical world is increasingly conceptualised as "made of information, with energy and matter as incidentals". Furthermore, our physical world has the remarkable property that the maximum information storage capacity of a system is bounded not by its three dimensional volume as one would expect, but by the two dimensional area of its boundary with *other* systems. This will not sound important to the uninitiated, but the consequences of this property are profound: *information storage capacity is determined by the set of relations it has with other storages of information,* **not** *the storage itself.* As a loose rule of thumb, this means that the more interconnected something is, the more information it can retain; and equally, should it lose its interconnectedness, it will lose capacity of retention.

How we ought to interpret this is unresolved, to put it mildly, and there has been a twenty year profusion of thought experiments in the literature trying to figure out what such a reality looks like and what testable hypotheses might result. In general in science, and especially at the cutting edge, and so long as no evidence or logic is contradicted, one can choose to interpret evidence as one chooses hopefully improving *lex parsimoniae*[6] wherever possible. I follow a very similar evolutionary least-action thermophysical opinion to Prof. Annila of Helsinki University[7], but I take it a step further by choosing to read the process of dynamically reconfiguring paths of information travel as a cognitively

---

[6] The Law of Parsimony, colloquially called 'Occam's Razor'.

[7] For example, Annila, A., (2011), 'Least-time paths of light', *Monthly Notices of the Royal Astronomical Society*, doi: 10.1111/j.1365-2966.2011.19242.x shows how the *ad hoc* conjectures of dark energy and dark matter can be dispensed with by utilising Maupertuis' principle to determine the least-time paths taken by light rays. This shows that an evolutionary interpretation of mechanics, which incorporates the changing relations within a system, provides a simpler, more powerful, explanation than the orthodox theory which assumes a static, unchanging Universe surrounding the light ray.

proactive rather than as a passive process. In other words, while information storage is generally accepted as keeping a history used to proactively choose how best to act in least-time, and that is equivalent to maximising as many relations with other information stores as rapidly as possible, I go further by ascribing this process to be identical in every way with cognition itself: *autopoesis*, as the technical name for this is known[8]. I dived into this extensively across multiple chapters in *Freeing Growth: Volume 1*, but assuming that by now I am currently hurting your head, it's easy to summarise: it takes an ongoing, proactive act of *cognition* to retain information about the past, and that this ongoing act of cognition is performed by all matter (stores of information) at every scale from infinitesimal to infinity at a Universe-wide scale. That seems to be sufficiently equivalent to God to me to justify mapping God as this mathematical concept, or at least useful for mapping what God *isn't*.

My second reason, extending the first, is that I found this choice made thinking through these proposals much easier, because there is a point in any large, complex design where logic breaks down and an act of faith must be taken (also known as the Chaitin theorem). It also more accurately reflects our group in St. Andrews where none of us were religious in the sense that we took much notice of the strictures of any organised church, but where we all believed in some form of God without His accompanying human church, and most of us were fairly sure that divine revelation occurs at least to some people. I suppose that makes us varying mixtures of theism and deism. From my own personal perspective, God never changes anything except for once at the very beginning after which He learned from His mistake. However God speaks to all things capable of perceiving light i.e. information. All things can therefore choose to take God's advice, and God will always answer any prayer asking for advice, but God will never cause the free will of any other thing to be reduced. Therefore, any prayers requesting something to be different are a waste of time. Far better to ask for guidance on how *I* can change something rather than asking God to change it for you.

The final two reactions I feel I ought to mention are those of total incomprehension and the view that these proposals are impossible to enact, so why waste time even considering them. The former is a particularly interesting one – a lot of people, indeed most of the St. Andrews group themselves, have

---

[8] Autopoesis literally means 'self-making', and comes from a body of theory summed up by the 'Santiago Theory of Cognition' by Maturana and Varela. The most accessible, though quite out-of-date, book describing this in context is Fritjof Capra's *The Web Of Life* (1997) which itself is an updated rewrite of Erich Jantsch's highly influential *The Self-Organizing Universe* (1980).

reacted to these proposals with incomprehension, either explicitly stated or not. Myself and Megan were visiting Sarah in York two weeks ago, and she likes to roll her eyes whenever she mentions "Niall's crazy ideas". Megan will quite frankly say that she doesn't get them at all, but can explicate in detail how she doesn't. And Johanna is very keen about some of the proposals, lukewarm about others, and implacably opposed to a majority of them.

However here is the interesting thing: they are familiar with each of the topics, all have an opinion on them, and in so doing they demonstrate a socio-cultural ownership of them. The overwhelming reaction of the general population is one of absolute *indifference* to *any* proposal which is too big to immediately comprehend-through-stereotyping[9] unless someone whose opinion they trust has told them what to think about it.

And of course, if you think about it, that's simply human beings for you. It takes effort to wrap your head around complex topics. It requires critical thinking skills, which our education system does its best to stamp out at as early an age as possible. It's simply easier to copy someone else's opinion and assume that if they're trustworthy then they're probably right. Only if a topic starts to have immediate and potentially severe consequences for you personally do *some* people invest the effort to make up their own mind. If those people happen to be nexus points in society, the new opinion spreads. Interestingly, studies show that if a critical threshold of ten percent of a population come to believe an idea fervently, a further 75% will adopt that idea as consensus within a generation (Xie, J. et al., 2011). This explains how Neo-liberalism (policies typically associated with Reagan and Thatcher) went from a fringe theory, almost semi-religious quackery, in the 1950s to become orthodoxy by the end of the 1980s. What started as a set of semi-thought-through ideas and proposals (much like those in this Manifesto) in the 1950s became rigourised with mathematics during the 1960s, philosophically and sociologically enshrined into the wider discourse during 1965-1975, and politicised from the late 1970s onwards i.e. one human generation. So, to those who think that such far out proposals are impossible to enact, I will say this: all that has happened before will happen again. Far stranger worldviews have been adopted by mankind before, and will be in the future.

---

[9]   Some   feel   that   this   is   a   sign   of   our   decline   e.g. http://www.nytimes.com/2011/08/14/opinion/sunday/the-elusive-big-idea.html?_r=2&pagewanted=all in which a New York Times columnist feels that young people, in particular, are no longer interested in big ideas with consumerism and hedonism having usurped any non-self ideology. Personally, I think that the big idea discourse is always limited to a tiny minority of the population, and where they used to discuss these things in the newspapers written by the elite for the elite, with mass media these discussions are now held and published elsewhere more exclusive as so to avoid being pilloried while doing so. For example, one such private forum would be within some undergraduates at universities such as St. Andrews.

How the Predictions have fared since 2008

So far the predictions are on course, but one projection we now know has changed considerably, which has deep and profound consequences on the recommendations made in this Manifesto. Back in 2008 I assumed that Peak Oil would occur sometime around 2015 and Peak Gas would occur sometime around 2030-2035. At the time, that was the best considered estimate of the International Energy Agency, so there was no reason to doubt it, and *Freeing Growth: Volume 1* was written assuming it would be so. We now know that because of shale gas, Peak Gas is likely to exceed 2050 assuming that the hype has some substance to it.

The most obvious consequence of this is as follows: where previously there was no real point in investing substantially in a gas based economy given the paltry fifteen year return, there is very considerably a point when there is a thirty plus year return. Energy investment generally follows a thirty-five year return on investment calculation, so if shale gas does extend Peak Gas past 2050 then I think it extremely likely that we shall transition from an oil based economy to a gas based economy, even though we merely postpone the inevitable transition to post-fossil fuels thereafter.

Thinking this through in terms of energy densities much as Appendix A in this Manifesto does, shale gas consists mostly of methane (natural gas) with some ethane (2-15%) and small amounts of butane and propane which are typically used to make Liquefied Petroleum Gas (LPG). Methane isn't economical to use for transport as it requires two hundred atmospheric pressures to liquefy and an impractically large combustion volume in order to be efficient, but LPG liquefies at just 2.2 atmospheres and is perhaps only 20-25% less efficient in engines than petrol. However, LPG is one third less dense by volume than diesel (26MJ/l versus 38.6MJ/l) and the added weight of its high pressure container is not insignificant, so LPG based transport is probably between twice and three times as energy expensive from refinery to kilometre travelled as oil based transport[10]. Nevertheless, it is still vastly better than hydrogen which I still think is simply impractical as well as deeply unwise (see Appendix A).

Such a change has multiple consequences. Where Haber-Bosch nitrogen fixation was going to collapse around 2025 (and therefore food supplies decline by about 85%), now it will occur a whole generation later. Interestingly, this

---

[10] It's too soon to say what the Energy Return On Energy Invested (EROEI) is for shale gas yet, but early estimates are between 50 and 70 times though it is presently thought with a 60-70% drop after one year of extraction. Given that oil has an EROEI of 15-20 in the Middle East, that suggests that shale gas driven LPG transport should be about as whole system efficient as oil transport – at least, at the start anyway.

doesn't prevent the two billion deaths predicted by this Manifesto because transport costs will still have risen so substantially as to make those lives unsupportable, simply because one cannot move the food from its sites of surplus (the US, Europe, South America) to the starving (Africa, India) at an affordable price. It does, however, mean that eutrophication of coastal regions will continue, much to the detriment of the biosphere there, as well as continually increasing contributions to the excess of carbon dioxide in the atmosphere with all the obvious consequences on the likelihood of fatally increasing the rate of the present mass extinction due to melting clathrates (Benton & Twitchett, 2003). And it does mean that Peak Phosphorous (which is absolutely necessary for crop growth) and the energy investment per potash extracted (ditto for crop growth) suddenly become vastly more important: 'easy' sources of phosphorus likely peaked in 1990 but the crossover with 'hard' sources may occur anywhere between 2030 and 2050 (White & Cordell, 2009)[11], and no one really knows about future supply constraints of Potash, though the recent bidding war for Potash Corporation, one of the largest holders of potash mining rights, has been telling.

I no longer have a set of bright young minds against which to bounce these ideas, so I have not attempted to modify this Manifesto in light of such substantial changes. Nevertheless, as I have said in this Manifesto, our accounting system was originally intended only as a temporary war time measure by the Normans because it was recognised even then as only being good for winning wars right now at the cost of your own future. The perpetual wars of medieval Europe made it the *de facto* accounting system, and capitalism discovered how to convert a war time accounting system into a prevailing economic system which extracts wealth as rapidly as possible for the least *human* cost today. So long as we keep this system where we wage war against our own future, we are all absolutely and totally screwed no matter what technologies we invent or anything else we do.

On that basis I reckon that while my predictions may not come true when I said they would, they still will come true.

---

[11] See also http://www.theoildrum.com/node/4624 for a discussion about 'Peak Easy Phosphorus' and 'Peak Hard Phosphorus'.

How the Proposals have evolved since 2008

An oft-asked question is what changes would I make to the proposals given the hindsight of three years? That is really two questions: (i) what have I been working upon since 2008 and (ii) what mistakes do I think I made?

On the latter, I would fill out a few of the proposals in greater detail sure – writing the book has improved my writing clarity no end, and additionally there are some small tweaks which ought to be made. I would additionally write Proposal 1 (Divorce the Money Supply) in Maths or computer program code both of which are far clearer than can be done in English. But apart from the problems introduced by shale gas outlined earlier, I can't say that I have since discovered any major flaws. To my knowledge, and indeed surprise, the proposals are generally as sound today as they were in 2008.

On the former, I have come full circle back to where this line of enquiry first began. A topic I very briefly mentioned in *Freeing Growth: Volume 1* was next generation linguistics where I advocated the design of a new, more powerful language for the ruling elites to speak and use as so to cement the legitimacy of their rule within post-fossil fuel civilisation. This language has the interesting feature of directly mapping onto topological mathematics, so one speaks (and therefore thinks) primarily in terms of transformations of collections of information and the flows of information which make up structure, just as is required by the Information Holography of Physics, Computers and Mathematics outlined earlier. I am no strong believer in the Sapir-Whorf hypothesis (that the structure of language determines thought), but I do believe that the increased awareness and ongoing refamiliarisation with state-of-the-art mathematical techniques would be highly conducive to enabling a higher rate of sustained growth. What better way, after all, of ensuring people's regular practice of mathematics than to make it the very language one speaks?

Usefully, and to ensure this new language does not end up like Esperanto, a subset of this language also functions as a functional computer programming language which operates a next generation computer software design which I began work upon back in 1994, and have about sixty-thousand lines worth implemented and running well. One therefore has an especial reason, as one aspiring to become one of the world elite within an authoritarian context, to learn and master this language as it also enables one to program computers which is surely a *sine qua non* of future eliteness. I suspended work on this computer software in 2004/2005 in order to undertake the human research necessary to sociologically enable this software whilst studying at St. Andrews, and from which the *Freeing Growth* book and this Manifesto was derived. I had originally hoped to return to developing it, but I now think that my efforts would be better invested elsewhere. In the end, the software can't be adopted by society until society is able to adopt it, and unfortunately history shows that substantial, society-wide changes are rare outside of dictatorships and in the face of widely recognised fatal threats. Preparing the ground for either or more likely both of these must therefore be my primary mission.

Much of my time since 2009 has been occupied with the necessities of earning money and attempting (unsuccessfully thus far) to establish a reliable source of income. I have also wasted a lot of time and effort applying for entry into doctoral study, unfortunately discovering no doctoral supervisor who is willing to take me at a university I can afford. As a result, I only get to work infrequently on the bigger plan of research which surrounds the proposals.

Still, in the next few years I do intend to learn Lojban − a constructed, syntactically unambiguous human language based on predicate logic − as I think it would be useful not just to me, but also to help shape the minds of my children in a way advantageous to them in the long term even if the language itself is fairly impractical as a 'daily driver'. As always, freeing personal growth never stops!

Niall Douglas
Cork, September 2011

If you liked this book, and would like to be kept abreast of Freeing Growth developments, please visit:

http://www.freeinggrowth.org/

... and join our Facebook page, subscribe to Freeing Growth news via RSS or Email, ask questions, and discuss anything related to Freeing Growth with other readers!

This book is dedicated to the following people,
who played their irreplaceable roles in the genesis of this book,
and to whom I owe most of my St. Andrews experience:

My father and sister, Francis and Aoife
Megan
Johanna

Sarah
Ingrid
Anneka

Natasja
Olga

McKinley
Katherine
Valentine

CHAPTER 1

Preamble

A spectre is haunting the world – the spectre of imminent collapse caused by a perfect storm combining severe environmental degradation, severe price inflation due to demand outstripping supply of fossil energy and the temptation towards tyranny in the name of centralised control called forth by panic. With the recent accession of the US, all the major powers of the World have entered into an alliance to exorcise this spectre: politics of the left and the right, countries of the East and the West, populations of rich and poor.

This alliance intends to save human civilisation through restraining human behaviour using a centralised bureaucracy. It intends to save us from ourselves through dictating carbon permits, setting quotas and signing binding international treaties, all in the name of reasserting power over a world perceived to be spinning out of control. Their intent is noble and laudable, but their method will only stave off the inevitable for the exact same reasons as why Communism failed, as did the Roman Empire, as have countless great civilisations of History.

We believe that the only solution which can save not just our civilisation, but also our planet is to embrace growth: to free ourselves, our economy and the free market to fix what it caused in the first place. We call our detailed plan for action *Neo-Capitalism*, which literally means 'New Capitalism'.

A True Free Market Capitalism

It is not fashionable to say this in the current zeitgeist, but the free market is the single greatest wealth generator ever invented in human history. As world governments return to Neo-Keynesian macroeconomic policies to stave off yet another financial meltdown, we believe that collapse comes from the misappropriation of our economic engine, not the generator of that wealth itself.

Our economy has been on a war footing for a millennium: it is programmed to extract as many material resources as possible for the least possible present cost to *humans* today – this is how we have perceived 'efficiency'. Yet this need not be the case: we could program it instead to maximise its internal rate of self-improvement which is identical to the maximisation of work extracted from the utilisation of energy. Such an economy rapidly invests long-term in biosphere productive capital rather than extracting it as human profits today; such an economy maximises the rate of long-term sustained growth rather than the unsustainable short-term growth of recent history. Such an economy betters and improves the lot of all mankind rather than condemn its majority to penury and involuntary servitude.

What does this mean? This means that such an economy grows at double-digit sustained annual rates whilst simultaneously repairing all the damage done to the biosphere, to such an extent that the biosphere is in a better state by 2050 than it ever was at any time in the last ten millennia. This means that where technological progress was slow and technological understanding was confined to an elite few, in such an economy technological progress is rapid and technological understanding is widespread and considered typical. Where at present we have no shortage of human ability and brilliant ideas but a complete lack of capability and successful entrepreneurship, in such an economy human capability more closely matches human ability and people directly receive what they earn for themselves. Where large sections of the richest peoples of the world have lost their connection with God, in such an economy God is placed at the centre of all human endeavours from large to small, thus restoring the great freedom which the Prophets gave our ancestors.

While we currently have notional freedom in much of the world, in reality our **practical** freedom of choice is severely constrained by ignorance, poverty, incapability and foolishness – all clear signs of distance from God. There are too many penalties for being creative and taking risks, and nothing like enough reward for entrepreneurship and failing successfully.

We believe that these proposals will free the individual, the group, the society and the world. Moreover, they have been deliberately designed so they can be implemented in part or in full: the further they are implemented, the higher the growth achieved. True liberty requires giving every person and group the right to choose: better behaviour comes from within, it cannot be imposed from outside, and these proposals are designed to be opt-in or opt-out where possible.

CHAPTER 2

Our Profile of the Coming Collapse

This is how we foresee the next few decades of human existence. If we are wrong, then ignore us. But mark our words: if we are proven correct, then heed our recommendations.

1. As demand for outstrips supply of natural resources (namely ores, minerals, fresh water and fossil energy), their price relative to the market shall rise. Much of this price rise has already occurred but has been hidden by market distorting subsidy which has created the false illusion of price stability.

2. The monies earned through natural resource extraction shall be reinvested into furtherance of the same, thus spurring ever increasing natural resource extraction as the great Economist William Stanley Jevons predicted in *The Coal Question* in 1865 (the 'Jevons Paradox').

3. The bubble shall become unsustainable, resulting in a collapse of the extraction cycle. Great wealth shall be lost, people will panic and look to the government to solve their problems.

4. Government takes on ever greater centralised control in dictating the economy, stabilising but not preventing the decline. The decline slowly gnaws away at civil liberties in the name of saving us all, slowly suffocating the creative spark which is the engine of any economy.

5. Civilisation crumbles. Billions die, some in wars [12] but most from hunger, and humankind returns to a Dark Age which takes hundreds of years to pass.

---

[12] See Appendix A on page 47 for more detail.

The first of the cycle collapses has occurred: that of finance which was entirely predictable and indeed was predicted for over a decade by many people indeed since the Enron debacle, including Nobel Prize winner Joseph Stiglitz. In response to the currency crises of the late 1990s, developing nations invested the wealth generated by their extraction of natural resources back into the West, causing a surfeit of cheap debt. This cheap debt propelled a property & finance bubble where as always with any speculative bubble, people began to believe that they could become wealthy without having to perform the work necessary to acquire that wealth (this is only ever possible for a parasitic minority, never more than that). As with all speculative bubbles, wealth was temporarily pushed into where it is not productive – namely under-skilled labour and the trapped wealth of real-estate – and therefore is an unsustainable inflationary misallocation of wealth.

To date, the solution which has been adopted by most Western economies is to borrow even more of the excess wealth which caused this problem to begin with, in order to fiscally stimulate their economies through grand government spending programmes. We predict that this solution will not work because this depression is **not** one of lack of demand as Neo-Classical Economics predicts, but rather one of **too much** demand given the dwindling supply. We predict that in fact this collapse is the first of a series of collapses as our civilisation goes into decline, and all that fiscal pump priming will achieve is massive rises in national debt and the return of high inflation as the excess liquidity washes out.

Our Prediction of the Near Future for the West

To be specific in our predictions, we believe that the world economy shall continue to decline in activity for another two years until around 2011 whereupon it shall stabilise but not grow despite all attempts to make it do so. By 2015 an increasing decline in the supply of fossil fuels combined with rapidly increasing ecosystem costs as vital sources of food & fresh water increasingly become unavailable shall begin a period of general price inflation which shall require substantial monetary contraction (i.e. a large rise in interest rates) to control, thus further contracting economic activity. Due to this general price inflation, pension funds shall lose between 40% and 60% of their real value which shall require retirees to return to work, adding millions to the workforce and therefore creating a mass unemployment problem in the West. We estimate that this should begin by 2020.

In the name of creating stability and already emboldened by the relative transfer of power to themselves from a shrinking private industry, governments shall become tempted to fully utilise the surveillance opportunities made possible by modern technology. Satellites shall be linked with mobile phone position monitoring to record the movements of every citizen in real-time (see Appendix A). Wherever there is networked information technology, there becomes possible a means of enforcing control of thought, movement, speech and motion. This will happen so slowly that few will notice: freedom shall become snuffed out by a thousand cuts. Meanwhile, people will become even more afraid of the very same technology which has fuelled our economic growth over the last thirty years – and thereby dooming Western civilisation to stagnation and decline.

Our Prediction of the Near Future for the Rest

Despite the loss of around half their purchasing power and living within a slowly decaying tyranny, the citizens of the West shall escape lightly when compared to the rest of the world. As Vaclav Smil (2001) has reported, at least two billion of the world's poorest shall become unsupportable due to food price rises (we estimate of between 400% and 800%) and shall have to perish, thus provoking widespread discontent and mass migration towards richer zones. This shall require the West to build exclusion zones by mining land & sea and erecting walls to keep the starving out. Meanwhile, despotic governments shall merrily expend the last resources of their poverty stricken nations on weapons of mass destruction, freely using them to murder tens of millions in the name of restoring control.

The worst famines should afflict (in order) China, then Africa, then India as these are the most dependent on fossil fuel inputs or imports for their food supply (especially drought prone Asia which heavily relies on pumping irrigation water around which is especially fossil fuel intensive) – however, even the hitherto breadbasket of the United States should become dependent on net food inputs just to feed itself as huge swathes of currently productive agricultural land become useless (and that's even assuming a mostly vegetarian diet unlike at present).

Despite how bad all this may look, we do not believe a third world war will begin for reasons outlined in Appendix A on page 79.

We appreciate that such predictions seem so dire as to be impossible. However, we have calculated these models on the best available science, and we are using the exact same methodologies as eminent researchers such as Lester Brown in his *Plan B 3.0: Mobilizing to Save Civilization*. Our sole difference is that we assume a more realistic vision of human nature based on historical real-world behaviour rather than (in our opinion) wishful thinking.

Having considered our likely near future, the question emerges: what are we going to do about it? What *should* we do about it?

CHAPTER 3

Our Proposals

Knowledge complicates. Understanding simplifies. We believe that in order to free growth, we must embrace the following philosophy, principles and worldview:

1. We are borne into slavery: the bonds of ignorance and irresponsibility. Ignorance stems from unfulfilled ability. Irresponsibility stems from not understanding the consequences of exercising capability. Freedom can ONLY be gained from depth of understanding and skill giving forth to capability. Responsibility can ONLY be gained from understanding capability, **therefore true freedom can only be *responsible* freedom**. As said by the Ancients, this truth and only this truth will set you free: he who has the capability to destroy the world, but chooses to not do so out of love, is closest to God. Such a person walks regularly in the Kingdom of God.

2. Self-improvement can ONLY come from within through love, perseverance and creativity. It can be aided, encouraged or cajoled from outside, but like love it can never be externally imposed without permission. An optimally growing society equals every single citizen growing at their optimal rate which can ONLY be achieved by each citizen and each group having the freedom to self-determine their own improvement, and to reap the consequences of that which they sow. One can never be dragged into the Kingdom of God: one must **earn** that admission.

3. It is a hard fact of thermodynamics that unstable complexity arises from the use of energy. In recent decades, we have been expending around four hundred times the amount of energy sequestered from the sun by the biosphere annually – it has become a physical addiction as our

waistlines have swollen grotesquely, our blood vessels have filled with an excess of fats, our bodies have become ravaged and our minds ossify far earlier than they should. Just as our bodies overflow with deadening complexity, our society and economy are equally suffocated by lack of powerful simplicity: witness our bureaucracies, our legal systems, our schools & universities, our financial systems and so on[13]. We are literally dying from too much deadening complexity dragging us down: the ONLY life-saving medicine is a heavy dose of powerful simplification.

4.   Analogously, we must accept that much of our *useful* energy supply is going to drastically reduce in the coming few decades[14]. All currently known alternative energy solutions: nuclear, tidal, geothermal or wind, cannot supply the hydrocarbons with which we run our industries and with which we feed, clothe and house ourselves. The good news is that the use of hydrocarbons generates most of the severe environmental degradation and most disease afflicting the West, so many of our systemic problems will shortly be curing themselves; the bad news is that no one can realistically imagine a modern world without hydrocarbons at its energy centre. A complex legal system which requires years to punish crimes and make decisions; a penal system which costs society more per serious offender than to raise an average child to twenty-one; a cumbersome intellectual property and behaviour regulation system which spends most of its time creating fear and apathy rather than promoting growth; a healthcare system which expends most of its resources on the dying rather than upon the future; an education system so inefficient that it consumes the most productive first third of a human's lifespan – all of these things are unsustainable things of luxury made possible ONLY by massive flows of energy. All of these luxuries are simply unaffordable after the fossil fuel supply starts to decline – and this is no matter how many electricity generating facilities we build, because electricity does not (cost effectively) generate hydrocarbons.

---

[13] Witness after all how many pieces of paper a person must nowadays obtain in order to do anything at all: everything requires some sort of certificate or however many extra years in expensive third level education whether the student requires the training or not. How insecure must we have become?

[14] See Appendix A on page 47 for the specifics on how we have assumed the fossil energy crunch will play out.

5. Lastly, we of Western tradition split the mind & body in order to split the atom: the history of Western civilisation since Descartes has been one of ever finer subdivisions. This has been our greatest strength whilst also our greatest weakness: we have both saved the world whilst simultaneously dooming it. This dichotomy is ONLY possible when one holds the paradox of mind and body being separate: form becomes separate from function, structure becomes separate from process, the individual becomes separate from society, the past becomes separate from the future. We both recognise the tremendous power of holding this paradox at the same time as recognising its tremendous curse: it allows man to glimpse the Kingdom of God whilst simultaneously never being able to step into it. How can this be remedied? We believe that the ONLY solution for the mind-body split is **to know thyself before all other things**: to know that you understand the split, what it means and doesn't mean, to realise that not acting is to act, to both believe and disbelieve in the true power of God, to render all and sundry as both identical and totally incomparable. All that has happened before is still to happen: so what are *you* going to do about it?

We believe that our future lies not in healing the mind-body division, but rather in *transcending* it. We believe that our future lies in successful failure, not failing to succeed. We believe that our future is the return to personal self-responsibility where the individual is supported by society, but is not created by society.

To that end, we quickly overview the following specific proposals which are detailed in the *Freeing Growth* series of books. We have taken many assumptions as a given in the following: see Appendix A for a list of some of these. The proposals roughly fall into four primary categories: (i) Economic (ii) Education (iii) Legal (iv) TBTI (Too Big To Imagine). Note that as far as possible any proposal stands as separate from the others as we have been able to achieve, but fundamentally we are taking a holistic approach where many small changes need to be performed to multiple parts of society simultaneously.

Our Economic Proposals

1. Divorce the Money Supply

We propose the division of the money supply into three separate types: (i) animate (ii) inanimate and (iii) human revenue. Animate money (€_a, $\$_a$ or $\pounds_a$) denotes the contribution to biosphere welfare of alive things e.g. cows, trees, humans, insects, bacteria and so on. Inanimate money (€_i, $\$_i$ or $\pounds_i$) denotes the contribution to biosphere welfare of material things e.g. rocks, houses, factories, oxygen and so on. Both animate and inanimate monies purely describe *productive capital*. Lastly, human revenue money (€_r, $\$_r$ or $\pounds_r$) is the human-valued revenue from the fruits of these two productive capitals – or what is more normally known as 'cash'.

For the vast amount of daily activity, one would not notice the difference as most goods transactions and almost all services transactions are in €_r[15] which is the normal everyday banknotes with which we are familiar. For example, purchasing a loaf of bread uses €_r money, as would attending a cinema or paying for house insurance. Even purchasing a small productive item such as a small computing device such as a mobile phone would probably be in €_r, however as a car is clearly a larger productive capital item it would be priced partially or wholly in €_i as would be a house or factory. As a clear example, to buy a farm would have three prices: a price in €_a for its livestock and agricultural capacity, a price in €_i for its machinery and buildings and a price in €_r to reflect goodwill (the human value ascribed as above and beyond a firm's assets during purchase).

Each of these monies has a floating exchange rate just like the US dollar does to Sterling or the Euro. How much €_i or €_a your €_r can buy will change over time according to supply and demand. Each money has its own interest rate and separate monetary policy, so for all intents and purposes they are separate currencies: it is simply that much as one must buy Sterling in order to do business in Britain, one must buy €_a in order to purchase a farm or €_r in order to buy a loaf of bread.

What possible benefit does having things in two or three prices bring? In quick succession:

---

[15] By this stage one gets the point of the notation, so I will use the euro symbol from now on for notational convenience. However bear in mind that any currency symbol can be used instead.

1. The central bank has **vastly** improved monetary and fiscal control because it can now tweak individual sections of an economy in order to promote growth and stability. For example, it could increase a tax on conversions into $€_r$ (as an exchange rate spread), thus inhibiting liquidations of capital into revenue but not inhibiting conversions of capital from one kind to another. Under this proposal, the old severe boom & bust cycle is greatly smoothed out in favour of gradual natural oscillations: a new era of high-growth stability hitherto impossible.

2. A brand new form of taxation becomes possible which involves no tax collectors, no invasion into privacy and where tax evasion is impossible: **the depreciation tax**. This is a simple flat tax (probably around 10-20%) on all revenue produced in an economy which is collected by the government simply printing excess $€_r$, thus causing deliberate (cash) price inflation. As all human valued revenue from productive capital must run through $€_r$, it taxes everyone and everything equally with no tax returns, tax collection or anything else required. Better still, the inflation strongly discourages holding money in cash, thus encouraging all saving as investment into productive capital.

3. It allows separate but concurrent domain accounting systems, as covered next ...

2. Divorce the Accounting System

Currently the best available proposal for reigning in excessive human behaviour (e.g. cutting carbon emissions or overfishing) is 'cap and trade' which involves some central bureaucracy setting some arbitrary quota upon production and letting an artificial free market exchange permits for a market determined price. Our major issue with this system is that it directly inhibits holistic solutions: the market is still programmed to maximise resource extraction so cap and trade simply creates disparate pockets which rarely if ever meet.

While we cannot currently see how fish quotas might interact with carbon quotas, we believe that the free market needs to be freed to find out. **Cap and trade is doomed to fail in the long term** – only a holistic reprogramming of the free market can possibly succeed. To this end, we propose separate accounting systems for our three types of money above, each of which feeds into the master profit & loss (P&L) account[16] which runs balances in each type of money.

Right now, most publicly listed corporations must publish their accounts annually or quarterly – this encourages short term optimisation at the expense of long term optimisation. Under our proposals, accounts are published *weekly* but with a confidence interval: this is a statistical likelihood of their accuracy which can be easily calculated by computer. All accounts are finalised after five years (for some particularly capital intensive industries this may be extended to ten or twenty years) at which point whatever remaining confidence interval is written off in order to draw a line under the accounts and therefore the performance of the firm. This proposal should prevent almost all of the accounting problems which have been dogging our corporations during the last few decades: the truth is that capitalism has sped up to be too fast for annual accounts to anything better than a figment of imagination. For example, the current credit crunch occurred because banks were in fact making losses since 2001 but their accounting systems had become substantially detached from reality. This proposal would prevent such extreme boom & bust enhancing behaviour caused by the accounts amplifying themselves over time.

The accounting system for $\mathcal{E}_i$ and $\mathcal{E}_a$ is calculated by computer according to the current best state of the art computer modelling, so a firm knows exactly what their net contribution to planetary welfare is in each of the three domains. This integrates into the economy the exact same scientific & empirically determined evidence as cap and trade does – however, it allows as much cross-domain quota optimisation as is theoretically possible. Therefore, unlike cap & trade which *has* to drag growth downwards on average, our proposal increases the sustainable rate of growth at the same time as repairing almost all the damage which has been incurred upon our biosphere.

3. Tax The Bad Things Which People Do, Never What They Earn

Why does government tax people's earnings which sends a signal that work and thrift is to be punished? We strongly believe in a wholesale realignment of taxation with natural social & moral forces by a massive expansion in what is euphemistically called 'sin taxes': *tax the bad things which people do, never what they earn.*

---

[16] This is the 'God P&L A/C' which has proven so controversial. In reality, it can be the 'Universe P&L A/C' or 'Master P&L A/C' if you so choose: so long as it encompasses all creation it can have any title you prefer.

We have provided above a mechanism for raising general taxes via the depreciation tax – the revenues from this alone is more than sufficient for running government. However, we recognise that losses to the $€_i$ and $€_a$ P&L accounts must directly affect $€_r$ in order to prevent conversion of natural capital into human revenue: therefore, we propose substantial sin taxes on unsustainable behaviour when performed by business. Governments however are ring fenced into directing[17] this revenue into investment into the biosphere to offset/prevent/ameliorate the damage in the first place. Despite what some on the left might say, to live is to cause death to other organisms and sometimes avoiding ecosystem damage is not the optimum path for the biosphere.

We do not believe in sin taxes for individuals as they are too small an economic unit to generate useful $€_{a, i \& r}$ accounts, and moreover any attempt to impose sin taxes upon something which is costly to monitor like an individual simply incentivises moral corruption in that person in attempting to circumvent the sin taxes (witness after all the criminal networks who subvert the tobacco sin taxes). We strongly believe that *imposing better behaviour upon people does not make them into better people*, and so we have a much better solution outlined below which unifies social & moral pressure with education (and at a very cheap price) which strongly encourages liberty. However, not everything lends itself to that scheme, and so therefore for the remainder of bad behaviour, sin taxes do apply to individuals as the sole form of individual taxation that any individual or business ever pays.

Remember: under our proposals, there are just TWO simple kinds of tax. The depreciation tax is the sole form of general taxation. The sole form of specific taxation is sin taxes placed on undesirable behaviour which damages the biosphere in some way and these mostly apply to businesses not people. **Most individuals and businesses will never individually pay tax under these proposals**: this is how you genuinely encourage and incentivise growth rather than the current schizophrenic approach of punishing what you say you want to encourage.

4. Divorce the Financial Markets

One of the greatest headaches facing publicly listed firms has been share price volatility which generates considerable shoe leather costs in capital maintenance and raises borrowing requirements. We propose the simple

---

[17] We do not intend by this that government should allocate the spending – rather we mean that these monies should enter a fund which supplies a free market specialising in the solution of these things.

solution of divorcing the investment market from the speculative market by restricting the trading of real shares to one day of the week (probably the day after when the weekly accounts are published). Meanwhile, buy and sell options are traded on a completely separate 24/7 derivatives market along with any other exotic financial instruments. One can still purchase from that derivatives market the right to purchase or sell a share at some given price in the future so the efficiency of capital allocation is maintained, however the firm itself need not worry about this: it is allocated the appropriate level of capital.

This should drastically reduce share price volatility whilst simultaneously reducing the costs of raising and maintaining capital – with a consequent decrease in the use of wholesale money markets for short-term credit (the current expense and scarcity of which is currently crippling industry). Capital markets are supposed to allocate capital according to risk, yet of late, due to securitisation, the risk has been disproportionately borne by financial services as a whole rather than upon the shareholder where it is supposed to be. If you would like the 'credit crunch' to be fixed so it will never happen again, this is a very good place to begin, and a far better approach than the use of even more borrowing using future taxpayers' funds as has been currently employed.

5. Divorce the shareholding structure

Currently if a shareholder uses insider information to dump their shareholding just before a firm becomes insolvent, they carry no penalty despite having had voting rights and therefore bearing some responsibility for that firm's behaviour. As any statistical analysis of the stock market will show you, sudden favourable share trades just before the announcement of especially bad (or good) news is extremely common which shows how endemic this problem of asymmetric information is[18]. We believe that not only does this moral hazard cause severe moral decay in the financial sector, it also severely impedes the efficient long-term allocation of capital to the detriment of long-term growth.

Furthermore, we also see a substantial problem in the current application of limited liability because it creates a further problem of moral hazard where shareholders do not take sufficient account of a firm's risky behaviour: in particular, speculators invest and divest with absolutely no thought given to the practices of what they are putting their money into. Limited liability pushes risk away from investors and onto other firms and society who must then absorb

---

[18] For example, despite the claim that the aircraft attack upon the World Trade Centre in New York in September 2001 was not anticipated, large movements on the stock market regarding the affected companies clearly shows that *someone* knew enough to make a very great deal of money indeed.

losses as we have just witnessed with the banking sector. This greatly increases the uncertainty of doing business and therefore inhibits growth – however, we do recognise that without any limited liability most investors would keep their money in the bank which simply transfers all the risk of investment onto the banks (which seems especially foolish at present because investors being so risk-adverse got us into this situation in the first place).

We propose another simple solution: modifying the share structure by divorcing ordinary shares into two types: voting and non-voting where voting shares have a variable limited liability (i.e. their liability ratio can be between 1.0 and say 4.0 of their investment value[19]) and that liability extends at a declining rate for a period of six months past the disposal of the investment. This allows institutional and individual investors who wish to only have indirect influence over the operation of the firm[20] to risk no more than the capital that they invest; equally, those who wish more direct influence must take on some additional risk to offset the added value of voting power.

It is expected that this one measure should greatly reduce the power of pension funds relative to individuals[21] who have been effectively shut out of publicly listed firms since the Second World War by the size of pension fund holdings – much as the great Economist John Kenneth Galbraith illustrated. This has allowed individuals to believe the patent untruth that corporations are separate and distinct from themselves, and that therefore that when a corporation murders some babies out in Africa that it does so because it is evil, rather than because the average Western consumer and pension fund would readily prefer cheaper chocolate bars over saving African babies. We believe that business must return to being loved and respected by every individual for strong growth to return: otherwise, 'public ownership' of the deeds of multinational corporations is impossible, and worker morale is sapped by anxiety from the internal conflict within the employees torn between doing well at their job and inflicting widespread suffering onto both man and nature.

6. Stop Fighting Nature

A very great deal of human effort is expended upon activities which fight natural forces. These are a waste of resources and are a luxury made

---

[19] We propose that this liability ratio may be altered in response to economic conditions by the central bank as a tool of economic stability.

[20] Needless to say, a large investor can have considerable indirect influence by threatening to divest their holding if certain things do not take place. This is no different to the present case.

[21] This is because pension funds and other institutional investors must by law reduce risk as much as possible – this implies that they would mostly hold the reduced risk voteless ordinary shares.

unaffordable by the coming hydrocarbon crunch. There are far too many of these in total to count, but we consider the most pressing general categories to be:

1. Breaking up monopolies in the name of promoting competition/Subsidising competition where a natural monopoly is proper.

2. Market distorting subsidies of stupid, even monumentally idiotic behaviours on a mass scale – we particularly think of agriculture here.

3. The provision of what should be local services by a centralised, usually national bureaucracy. This particularly affects corporations (e.g. food miles), not just government.

4. The use of legal remedies for moral, social and personal issues which strongly incentivises and therefore generates endemic moral corruption.

Despite that wholesale destruction of vital biosphere services is the clearest example of us fighting Nature, and therefore of us fighting ourselves out of sheer spite, unlike many on the left we feel that the removal of cheap hydrocarbons will remedy almost all the most important of these problems. As an extremely simple example, overfishing much past the coasts becomes extremely hard without hydrocarbons. Equally, marine eutrophication and land desertification become much harder without cheap hydrocarbons to generate the excess nitrates. We are not saying that we should do nothing and let the imminent hydrocarbon scarcity fix all our problems – we are saying that we have far more pressing issues and to be honest, Nature will heal herself very quickly indeed if she is given a chance[22].

We specifically tackle the above four most pressing categories of us fighting Nature in the coming proposals. In particular, we see great opportunities for profit and substantial sustained increases in growth if we take economic, social and moral advantage of natural phenomena.

7. Enable conversion of monopolies into consumer governed cooperatives

The Rochdale Principles laid out the concept of a non-socialist consumer owned cooperative as distinct from socialist worker cooperatives – we propose the creation of a closely similar new kind of economic entity: the consumer

---

[22] There is this great belief that Nature is somehow delicate. This is utter bunkum – Nature is extremely robust. It is *we* who are delicate because a minor sneeze of the biosphere would eliminate almost all human beings overnight.

governed cooperative which is a fusion of a consumer owned cooperative with a traditional shareholder owned corporation.

The consumer governed cooperative is one where all voting shares are held by consumers in proportion to their trade with the firm (thus leveraging the divorcing of the shareholder structure proposed above) – therefore, the customer literally controls the firm and moreover, receives dividends according to their proportion of trade with that firm (though none of the liability). This eliminates the possibility of consumers being abused or ripped off by a firm because any excess profits are returned as dividends, and should a consumer governed cooperative really abuse its consumers then they can literally replace the Board of Directors.

A consumer governed cooperative can come into being through being initially incorporated as such or by any publicly or privately owned firm putting it to a vote of its shareholders. However, we go one step further: we propose the elimination of almost ALL regulatory requirements for larger consumer governed or owned cooperatives because such firms implicitly do not require external regulation – this provides a significant incentive towards conversion for all large and complex firms, particularly multinationals many of whom are bigger than the governments which try to regulate them.

We furthermore make one additional proposal: that any larger[23] privately or publicly owned firm can be converted to a consumer governed cooperative by plebiscite of its customers. We propose this on the basis of the success of democracy: the population have 'one big stick' which they can wield once every four or so years, and if it works for something as big as government then it certainly will work for a multinational corporation. We believe that a far improved way of ensuring outstanding customer service by monopolistic firms is to give its consumers a similar kind of big stick to wield should things become particularly bad – meanwhile, intrusive regulation can be dispensed with for the most part as it is inefficient, expensive, generates considerable uncertainty, wastes resources and incentivises moral corruption and deviousness.

All these proposals when combined particularly remove the need to prevent mergers, regulate behaviour or artificially introduce or prevent competition: all of which fights natural behaviour and wastes resources. Far better to let

---

[23] We use 'larger' in this proposal to mean a firm with a lot of regular customers – say more than 10,000 – and that no one customer exceeds 40% of sales. As covered in the *Freeing Growth* books, consumer owned or governed cooperatives are a bad fit for smaller firms or highly innovative firms or industries: they only really suit big, mature industries which tend towards oligopoly or monopoly.

consumers and larger firms regulate themselves without external intervention – this proposal helps to enable this.

8. Let people look directly after one another

Currently most nations employ some mix of nationally subsidised and privatised health service; elderly & poverty provision; schooling; welfare; transport, energy, telecommunications & water infrastructure and so on. All of these are natural monopolies due to one of:

1. Extremely high fixed capital requirements (e.g. laying cables).

2. The long lag time between doing a behaviour and paying for its consequences (e.g. smoking tobacco, overeating).

3. The public good nature of the facility. A public good is one where it is hard to get the many individuals who could make use of the facility to pay for it e.g. a fireworks display.

These 'big' services are highly valued by society and therefore are highly regulated and usually heavily subsidised from the public purse – however, they also tend to be hard to charge people the direct cost in an obvious way: to expand upon the above example, how many people would feel happy charging a terminally ill tobacco smoker their direct costs at the point of illness? One might feel that as a point of principle that they should persecute the ill in order to dissuade others from following a similar path, however we feel that no right minded person would much like the reality of it in practice. Compassion is an underrated virtue, yet by spreading out these costs onto everyone regardless of their behaviour simply rewards stupidity and punishes looking after yourself.

To this end, we propose that consumer owned or governed cooperatives should fill the gap. Government has no business involving itself into welfare, healthcare, schooling, elderly & poor or any other issue which is a *local concern*. Communities need to organise themselves to look after themselves – of course, government has a role in promoting and ensuring a locality doesn't keep putting things off e.g. a particularly severe name & shame sin tax may be applied to a locality which won't organise its own welfare system or won't provide for its poor (and by the way that sin tax is simply taken away and not refunded). And of course government has a role in ensuring that a local cooperative does not become protectionist by ensuring that its structure is orientated towards meritocratic growth rather than providing pork for local friends & relatives – in particular, government can guide and illuminate by helping ensure that cooperatives share and distribute their knowledge widely[24].

Many will quite rightly be alarmed at this point as we appear to be ignoring the dangers of too many large localised cooperatives: after all, the single most notable feature of the last century has been the ever increasing transfer of power and resources towards ever larger centralised bureaucracies (e.g. the EU in Europe and the Federal Government in the US). This has done much to eliminate the parochial inefficiencies of the past where local power gave into local concerns thereby grossly distorting the free market and deeply inhibiting growth – however, it has also created a sense of alienation in people from their local communities which has not helped to inspire them into taking initiative. We acknowledge Isaiah Berlin's concepts of positive and negative liberty[25], and we believe that Western civilisation has experienced too much negative liberty.

In truth, we would be far more concerned with the suffocating dangers of too many big cooperatives if it were not for our education proposals below. Given the revolutionary & extremely disruptive nature of these education proposals which empower people with skills, capability and creativity, we believe that outsourcing these big public services from government into the inherent conservatism of local cooperatives is a very important, perhaps vitally so, stabilisation mechanism without which all the excess creativity would destabilise and likely destroy our civilisation.

We freely admit however that we are cranking up both the explosive and restraining elements in parallel under the assumption that the two will sort one another out. This assumption is not taken for granted and is explored in detail in the *Freeing Growth* books.

---

[24] One way is to force each locality to swap say 5-25% of its operations with neighbouring localities. Neighbouring localities tend to be the most opposite e.g. wherever you find a particularly poor area there is usually a particularly rich area nearby. Such disparities are an untapped goldmine for enabling a system to regulate itself naturally without needing external inspectors.

[25] These concepts alone are worth a book or two, but in short negative liberty is where the individual has total freedom so long as they don't change much around them. Positive liberty is when an individual has the freedom to gain a group following sufficient to transform an entire civilisation. Due to the threat of Communism, the latter has been severely curtailed throughout Western civilisation during the last century. Cooperatives particularly enable positive liberty when compared to privately owned profit seeking firms because they inspire the belief in individual consumers that they can make a difference to the big firms from which they buy.

9. Eliminate all specific legal regulation for those which disclose all internal functioning

One thing implicit in any consumer owned or governed cooperative is that the public effectively have complete access to the internal workings of the business because it doesn't make much sense for it to be otherwise (after all, the owner has a right to know how their business operates, and if the owners are lots of people then there isn't much point in marking something as confidential). This sense of openness is particularly noticeable in the UK's Cooperative Group which is the world's largest consumer owned cooperative – yet it certainly hasn't impacted strategic success nor profitability even with the credit crunch.

We strongly feel that regulation simply creates an incentive to obscure your activities just in case you are breaking some law (the law has become so complex that it has become extremely hard to know if you are behaving legally or not). Hiding one's activities inhibits the dissemination of innovations and learning from the mistakes of others across wider society and is therefore a major drag on growth – therefore, we propose the killing of many birds with one stone by proposing the elimination of almost all regulation for those companies which disclose ALL internal functioning to the public.

When we mean all, we really mean all: we mean every email, memo, fax, letter, telephone call, account, web page visit, list of customers – the lot. We even expect that cameras are fitted internally which observe and broadcast the internal functioning of the firm live on the internet, that all employees are tagged with location aware microphones (which can be temporarily disabled by the wearer if needs be) and furthermore that a history of all this information is kept on a public server for a given time period, say for a minimum of six months with the more important material held for up to ten years.

This allows academics, researchers, competitors and most importantly of all, the company themselves to study the firm's performance and behaviour. Why does one firm (or a department or subsection within a firm) find some magic secret to rapid growth and success and yet a dozen others fail? Is it truly down to having the right calibre of people in the right place at the right time as is so often assumed, or it is more a matter of organisational culture, or visionary management? The truth is that no one actually knows: despite the pages of the Harvard Business Review being stuffed with all sorts of fancy academic theories, there is also a very obvious lack of substantial empirical evidence. If we want to truly free growth, we need sufficiently intimate access to the workings of business for study, and this proposal is vastly more useful in getting to the nub of things than balanced scorecards or personnel interviews.

This proposal rewards firms and their employees for making themselves 'naked' by removing the onus of regulation. This is possible because when any customer can literally review the case of mistreatment of some other customer, there really isn't any need for enforcement of legal rights as the free market provides succour. Should a company consistently mistreat its customers, the evidence will be plain to see for anyone and customers will go elsewhere – and so will employees should management mistreat them (actually it is more likely it will be that bad managers will be shown for what they are, and thus they must leave rather than the workers).

Many will say that this proposal is untenable because of the intrusion into workers' privacy – yet we feel that the privacy problem arises when management has exclusive access to such information and therefore use it to abuse and bully employees. When *everyone*, including your relatives, friends and strangers, has access to as much information as everyone else then it becomes a different problem entirely. We extend this proposal much, much further later on – meanwhile, this more limited proposal stands separate from what is proposed later.

Our Education Proposals

10. Invest education where it has most effect

We expend a lot of resources on education: most parents will remember making personal sacrifices for the benefit of their children especially when they were young and the parents were relatively much poorer. Most children in the West must compulsorily attend school until sixteen, or increasingly eighteen, whereupon the more wealthy ones will attend university until twenty-two (or even twenty-four with the rise of postgraduate qualifications) – throughout this time, most children are not productive members of society despite being in their prime of creativity and ingenuity (as any parent of an inquisitive and energetic three year old can tell you!). Wherever you go in the West, the average cost to raise a university-educated child tends to roughly approximate the cost of an average house – no wonder then that the birth rate has slumped and that couples wait until their thirties to begin despite the severe negative effects that this can have on the child's and their own health.

The tremendous problem with mass education is that it is mind-bogglingly inefficient: because a class of twenty to thirty trapped inside a room must proceed at a standardised rate broadly determined by the examination system, the brighter pupils are so underutilised that they often turn to destructive behaviours such as promiscuity and drug abuse in an attempt to mitigate the boredom, while the less able students become disruptive out of frustration. We like to pretend that school today is rather like when we were children, but this is a rose-tinted utopian fantasy: much like contemporary music videos, school today mostly consists of a cynical dog-eat-dog jungle where violence and sexual objectification abounds: in particular, the rate of sexual abuse of students (and even teachers) *by* little children is skyrocketing across the Western world, and the only reason that we can think of why this is not more widely acknowledged by society must be a profound denial of the evils which we must have done to cause a seven year old to rape other children.

As the *Freeing Growth* books illustrate, these patterns and experiences are repressed by many of our most successful students such that the A-grade students who win access to the most elite universities find a world pregnant with systematised date rape, deeply unhealthy compulsive behaviours and a level of coercive group denial which bodes very poorly for our collective future. No wonder after all that our corporations strip-mine the resources of the natural world when their elite executives strip-mined the resources of their school & university experience: at best our mass education system generates cynical psychopaths who are extremely adept at fooling others (after all, what else can a system based on fooling examiners do?), at worst it leaves our young disenfranchised, incapable, ignorant and dependent on welfare for the rest of their lives.

We acknowledge that mass education has succeeded in one single area: it has achieved a fairly universal capability in reading & writing, and that one capability has contributed very significantly to economic, social and personal growth without which the 20th century could not have been. However, that gain concluded itself some thirty years ago now – since then, the average member of society is as ignorant & incapable today as they were thirty years ago (and on some measures such as general awareness they are significantly worse). We therefore take the position, considering the empirical evidence, that **the mass education system has failed** in its primary purpose of educating society. We therefore propose a complete & total replacement of the education system in its entirety.

Our primary observation is that we know from mountains of evidence that children have learned more than half of what they will **ever** know by the age of **five**. Why therefore do we invest a tiny fraction of what we put into third level universities into the education of the under-fives? From the scientific evidence that is a tremendous waste of resources and moreover is mostly a tax funded subsidy of the middle classes and multinational corporations. If continued, this astonishing misappropriation of resources will ruin us.

We therefore propose first & foremost that five percent of our economy be allocated exclusively to the education of the under-sevens. Class sizes should not exceed three maximum per teacher and classes should begin from the age of between three and six months old (which empirical studies have shown is by far the best time to teach children mathematics). We explain our proposals in much greater detail in the *Freeing Growth* books, but the **minimum** that we expect upon completion of school at the age of seven is that every child can read, write, understand mathematics to a topological level[26] AND teach themselves new skills through self-directed research.

---

[26] A topology is like an abstract stretchy sheet which you can manipulate: it is currently considered much harder than calculus (indeed, calculus is a prerequisite of topologies), in fact one currently needs to study maths at a postgraduate level to really sink one's teeth into topologies. In order to instil this into the general population, it will require a significant reworking of how mathematics is taught: away from the arcane symbolic notation used at present in favour of a holistically integrated *practical* approach where **every** subject, indeed everything in life, is approached from a non-linear fractal topological perspective much as animals and indeed ourselves naturally do as part of being perceiving the world through cognition. One need not be able to manipulate arcane symbols to understand and perform mathematics; equally we need to stop fighting our natural predilections by imposing an unnaturally abstract method upon the student.

Many think that such a standard is so high as to be comical. We have found a strong correlation between the intensity of their mockery and their emptiness as a human being. No one who has witnessed the tremendous power of a child at play can be anything less than shamed with how we waste its potential. In particular, we realise our age most pertinently when a four year old runs mental rings around us – anyone who does not realise this at the time is impoverished.

From the age of seven onwards children ought to be available to the workforce: seven year olds have an abundance of energy and they should be working in the low end repetitive and labour intensive jobs for which children are ideally suited. Indeed, children have always worked from this age onwards throughout human history: we only very recently stopped the practice as part of our campaign against child exploitation in general. This Victorian-era myth of the carefree and innocent childhood is a luxury made unaffordable by the coming hydrocarbon crunch – whether we enact this proposal or not, children will have to return to work as civilisation decays and we would greatly prefer avoiding a return to child exploitation.

We most certainly do not propose a return to the child workhouses of old. No, the next proposal reforms what work is in the first place and not just for children, but for everyone.

11. Grow harder rather than working harder

Our next proposal is perhaps even more radical than putting seven year olds to work: we know from mountains of empirical evidence that creativity requires free time, not just to implement an idea but also to come up with it in the first place. We also know that creativity is generated primarily by experiencing disruptive thoughts and is hampered by excessively repetitive routine. If we truly want our society to maximise its growth, we **have** to tackle the lack of successful creativity in our society.

To this end, we propose that income tax begins no earlier than after twenty hours of work or its equivalent per week – in other words, if you work for twenty hours or less, you pay no income tax. *Tax the bad things which people do, never what they earn.* There is nothing stopping anyone working forty, sixty, eighty or more hours a week, however for multiple reasons it is an unproductive behaviour for both themselves and society and therefore it needs to be taxed as a sinful behaviour.

And what should they do for the remainder of their time if only working for twenty hours per week? We propose that they be paid out of the depreciation tax to educate themselves in new skills, so if a person wishes to maximise their earnings then they would spend twenty, maybe twenty-five hours per week working and the remainder taking skills-based examination modules in order to gain qualifications in the practice of various skills. Obviously these modules pay more for harder and more desirable skills, but they also pay more for higher grades (we propose a market driven allocation system which dynamically adjusts the pay per module according to market conditions, so while there is a lag between adjustment of pay and the needs of society, society does not want for the correct kind of skilled labour for long). There is no minimum or maximum time period for which to gain a skill qualification: progress is as fast or as slow as the student wishes. Some students may be able to handle five or six skill qualification modules simultaneously; others may prefer one at any given time. Most importantly these skill qualification modules need to be short: we have suggested a preferred maximum of roughly eighty hours of study per module. This corresponds roughly to one month, and we have proposed that the examinations are held at the end of each calendar month (except December).

Therefore our seven year old being almost entirely unskilled relative to other workers would get the lowest paid jobs, and therefore has a high incentive to gain skill qualifications because these pay a lot more relative to other work – in fact, most seven year olds would likely work only a few hours per day because studying is a far more economically productive use of their time especially considering the potential gains in future earnings. The better they are at teaching themselves new skills, the more rapidly their income will rise both in their job and the higher the price of skill modules available to them. Unlike the present school system, each student can proceed at their own pace and more importantly, they can take whichever subjects they find the most interesting which is a significant incentive for study.

Where do teachers, schools and universities fit into this? Without doubt the social element to learning is extremely important and we do not doubt that most students will struggle to teach themselves the finer points of a skill without an experienced instructor to help. The student is being paid on the basis of skill gained and grade received and we see no reason why an instructor could not be given a cut of that payment in return for services rendered. We believe that government introduced mass education for the best of intent, but its bureaucratic execution has severely stymied good education where there is every incentive to do the minimum possible and very little incentive to customise teaching for the student (i.e. students are made to conform to 'the programme' rather than vice versa).

We go far further into detail in the books, but we do not believe that universities are doomed under these proposals despite that, if successful, our proposed system obviously eliminates the need for any formal third level education system in its entirety. We admit that our models show that between two thirds and three quarters of universities shall have to close and the scope of the remainder shall become greatly curtailed. However, these closures have nothing to do with these proposals – the same proportion will close anyway after our civilisation has completed its descent because as we have said so often already, the current 'obese' third level education system is a luxury only made affordable by cheap hydrocarbons, a wish to subsidise the children of the politically important middle class and a bribe for the R&D departments of multinational corporations. Thanks to its selection system (actually an 'exclusion of anything different' system), most of its academics are incapable of anything other than incremental creativity, and successful entrepreneurship is severely misdirected into internal politicking. Imagine how many lecturers nowadays could earn their salary purely through spontaneous donations given by their students on the basis of their lecturing ability, as it used to be before the first World War? Even the good lecturers barely hold a room for more than a few minutes due to the typically dire presentation of irrelevant material. We are long overdue a substantial correction of demand & supply in this part of the education system, and that correction will come no matter these proposals. We are confident that what survives of university will become a beacon of blue-sky innovation which enables man to reach his potential. We even predict that the primacy and public high esteem of university, as professed in the 19th century by Cardinal John Henry Newman, shall be restored unlike the public derision and scorn it currently so rightly invokes.

12. Enskill, never teach

How many of you are just as good with mathematics are you were when you left school? One of the most staggering things about our mass education system is that it effectively dumps you at the end of it: thus where the student was once reasonably capable, through lack of practice they quickly lose their capability and ossify in almost every area. What is the point of proceeding through all those years of schooling if one forgets almost all of what one learned? No wonder that ignorance, fear, inability and stupidity abound at every level in our society: we all have a profound insecurity that we are no longer as good as we once were, and that perhaps we do not deserve what we earn. When combined with overwork, this translates into obesity, heart disease, anger, hatred and all the stress-related diseases which epitomise our society.

The simple solution is to expire skill qualifications after a period of time, without which one is no longer entitled to the job which that qualification allowed. As aforementioned, we have proposed a free market based skill module setting system which attempts to match the curriculum of each skill module to what society needs and is capable of over time, so skill modules change far more rapidly than at present. Under our new education system, this requires all citizens to regularly retake a given subject area over time which achieves two things: firstly, it keeps every member of society as fully up-to-date with the state of the art as possible whilst not exceeding their particular ability, and secondly it both maintains the capability within that person and *self-confidence* in that ability over time. One maintains a wide spread of capability such that the perverse problem of graduates in Mathematics being no longer capable of simple arithmetic disappears forever.

We propose a hierarchy of interlinked skill modules which become more and more interdependent as difficulty increases. Towards the top of our hierarchy the skill modules become increasingly creatively based in order to guide students towards the generation of practical innovations which synergise the universal patterns which weave our Universe together. We take the view that our best students should be the most creative AND practically useful entrepreneurs possible, who actively contribute at every level to economic, spiritual and philosophical freedom and growth. Too often at present it is culturally more sensible to not rock the boat: such a society can never grow quickly.

We go considerably further in this concept of limited lifetime skill qualifications later on in our proposals regarding Law: in particular, we advocate earning the right to freedom before freedom can be exercised.

13. Incubate **successful** creativity

One cannot instil successful self-directed entrepreneurial creativity into the under-sevens without tackling the whole environment of the young child: the younger the person, the more their mind roams free and picks up on things which adults can no longer perceive. Too often the efforts of a successful teacher will be ruined by any one or more of parents, siblings, peers or indeed other teachers. The ONLY way to maximise a child's capability is to optimise all of that which surrounds the child. Moreover, there is a severe time limit upon this process: if you haven't succeeded by the age of seven, then you are highly unlikely to do so later on no matter the resources invested (note however that what is instilled before the age of seven can take decades to emerge – as any victim of child abuse can tell you).

We are very certain that almost all new parents-to-be would elect to undertake child-rearing skill qualifications in the months preceding the birth of their first child and indeed would likely carry on with more advanced modules as the child ages. Unlike at present where fifty hour plus working weeks are common for both parents in white collar Western families, under our proposals parents have the free time to participate in the raising of their children – with much of the anger, frustration and stress of overwork removed. Unlike at present where parents are often locked into undesirable job positions and career paths, under our proposals they have more than ample opportunity to improve their prospects through self-education, starting a new business or even taking a second job on a trial basis without having to hide the extra hours they are working from their current employer. Imagine already the profound improvements to morale, worker allocation, productivity and the reductions in costs to business caused by sickness, depression, training costs and burnout.

We have particular issue with the current orientation of the examination system around theory rather than **personal** practice: this alienates the student from their education in a way which appears to us to be intended to generate a barrier from the successful exercise of practice, and therefore successful entrepreneurship. For example, successfully telling lies and getting away with it is a cornerstone of success in Western civilisation, yet have you ever seen a class teaching practical lying skills? Where are the classes teaching critical thinking, a capability so devoid in graduates that it truly beggars belief? While Shakespeare's writing illuminates the English language with grace and wisdom, what direct relevance does his writing have to the teenagers forced to study his works? If you wish to destroy any passion for the English language in the majority of students, the typical Western English school curriculum is almost perfect. The same certainly goes for the 'hard facts' based History curriculum whose irrelevancy is guaranteed to put off most of its students from ever touching History again: perfect for enabling students to forever more repeat the mistakes of the past. No wonder then that we have driven our planet into a death spiral, our morals into the pits of Hell and that we systematically murdered more people during the 20th century than in all of preceding human history combined.

We say this: to incubate **success** means instilling into our young the capability to successfully **fail** again, and again, and again until the Eureka moment occurs. This is currently considered the exclusive purview of the scientist and the businessman: we say that this above all needs to be a universal capability.

The ideal human being is someone who has the power to destroy all which surrounds them, yet possesses the wisdom and understanding to know that growth is best optimised by leaving things alone (apart from an occasional nudge). Such is the Nature of God Himself: true freedom equals knowing to NOT make use of the power of God, because true freedom can only result from not denying another's freedom. Our insecure obsession with control and domination equals an obsession with short-term success which is the guaranteed path to long-term failure. Only through embracing success at short-term failure can long-term success become possible, and only through this can we ever find security within ourselves and therefore the salvation of present human civilisation.

14. Replace Intellectual Property with Central Ideas Database

The single most notable characteristic of any burgeoning civilisation is always a sudden flourishing of new ideas. To date, Western civilisation more than any other in history has liberated the dissemination of ideas: it is the foundation stone of our culture and unparalleled success.

Yet ideas are dangerous because **ideas unpredictably transform that through which they pass**. We agree that ideas need to be controlled, however we struggle to think of a system of control worse for growth than the concept of Intellectual Property. We have little problem with Trademarks: these are useful. We have considerable issue with Patents which tend to inhibit growth more than they promote it – and furthermore, the patent system is grinding very obviously to a halt in recent years under the sheer weight of patent litigation. Our greatest difficulty however lies with Copyright which we hold as one of the most insidious, dangerous, unhealthy and stupid ideas to have ever been invented by mankind. Our economic modelling shows that were it not for Copyright in computer software alone, average Western economic growth would have been one third higher since 1980. To put that in perspective, that equals the not insignificant addition of between ten and fifteen percent of those unemployed to the workforce since 1980.

The main cause of these problems is the high initial but near-zero replication cost of Intellectual Property: unlike physical property which creates scarcity the more it is replicated, Intellectual Property creates scarcity by a *lack* of replication. This is a perfect example of our economic system fighting its natural self: more economic resources have been wasted on this one internal conflict during the 20th century than in both World Wars put together.

Our solution is radical but cheap to implement: we propose a central ideas database where people can place ideas and content such as movies, music, books, art etc. People can then download as much or as little content as they please with part of the depreciation tax paying the most popular producers of content and ideas. For example, if someone uploads the design for a revolutionary new kind of improved pump, its designer is paid proportionate to the total economic contributions made by the use of that pump. This contribution can be calculated thanks to the divorced system of accounting outlined above, but also because by making the content free one aligns natural social tendencies towards sharing with increasing economic growth. Gaming this system becomes only possible when one person can pretend to be many other people, and that is only possible because our information security infrastructure is so appalling.

In a truly free society it should be extremely easy to be anonymous but extremely hard to imitate another. Our increasing paranoia and confusion of anonymity with insecurity, or secrecy with power, or security with anything but, is purely because of the half-arsed implementation of information security protocols within our society: for example, no matter how much information one possesses, it simply should not be possible to gain access to another person's bank account without their prior approval. Equally, it should not be possible to fake a communication from another person, nor ever use another person's computer data without their prior approval. Simultaneously, it is currently too difficult to electronically send information to another completely anonymously, with all the obvious incentives for tyranny this creates. If left unchecked, we wholeheartedly believe that these problems will eventually destroy our civilisation from within.

How we propose to fix these problems is several books in themselves, but in essence it involves reorientating our information structures at a deep and profound level. Currently information is held separate from that which interprets it: a mind-body distinction, and the source of great insecurity and wasting of growth potential – our proposal does some very interesting things in reuniting information with its potential. Douglas Engelbart began to show us the way in 1968: yet look at how poorly we have implemented his vision since. It is becoming time to knock the breadth of vision far beyond Engelbart's: we can propose a solution which truly maximises the potential of human effort, but it will require others to fully realise it[27].

---

[27] That said, we have a few ten thousand lines of programming code ready to go. See http://www.tnrev.org/ for more details.

Our Legal Proposals

15. Keep the Law Fresh

Politicians obtain and maintain their employment through popularity with their voters: it is however not a job which necessitates intelligence, knowledge or even ability. Because of this, politicians rarely write the text of the laws which they enact – even if they had the spare time, few possess the capability to write Law well, so this function is usually performed by special interest groups, a civil service or a politician's legal staff. Unfortunately, Law being Law, there is a definite tendency towards tedious verbosity and politicians, like most ordinary people, are often defeated by the sheer scale of Law.

Hence, we have landed ourselves in a most unfortunate predicament: (i) there is far too much Law in force for any one human to even remotely hold in their head at once, hence (ii) Law is falling increasingly into disrepute because few know whether they are breaking the Law (or not) so it becomes a matter of proceeding anyway and paying the fine *if* caught, thus (iii) the Rule of Law is breaking down, our prisons are swelling, our corporations (usually inadvertently) make a mockery of justice and the average educated person has never physically laid eyes upon a legal text even once. This obesity of Law, and it IS a disease clogging the arteries of economic growth just as much as a human heart, will suffocate human civilisation if we don't do something profound about it soon.

Our proposed solution is a hefty dose of powerful simplification: in particular, to stop adding even more Law to an already swollen rulebook because more is not always better. We propose that we enable politicians to actually know what policy they are setting by restricting the length any Law passed by them to just two thousand words: a *legal directive* rather than a legal specification. Furthermore, we propose that all the Law of a land be restricted to just four hundred thousand words, or one fairly large book which anyone can read and fully comprehend. If new Laws are passed which cause the word count to be exceeded, then they cause the automatic expiry of the oldest Laws in the four hundred thousand word corpus: this encourages lawmakers to intentionally expire Laws as they set new ones rather than the current situation of constantly adding even more Law to those currently in force. Even if a Law isn't expired in this fashion, it may well be wise to always have an automatic sunset provision in all Laws of no more than twenty years in order to ensure that Law always remains current and appropriate for present circumstances.

We recognise the no doubt horror that such a proposal will bring to the Legal Profession: we will be accused of destroying the basis of Western civilisation. However, nobody can respect the Rule of Law if nobody can *understand* the Rule of Law: most of the criminals seen by our courts have absolutely no idea of which specific crime they are guilty nor its potential punishment. Everyone knows that murder is wrong, yet only a handful of citizens know what the punishments for each degree of murder is – no wonder then that the would-be criminal is not disincentivised from committing the act! We can think of no better dissuasion from premeditated criminality if any would-be criminal could open the master book of Law and see for themselves exactly what the punishment would be. Equally, what better inspiration towards initiative when one does not fear unknown legal consequences!

If you might think this proposal impossible due to needing more Law than we have allowed for (e.g. through international treaty commitments), remember that earlier proposals have eliminated almost all regulatory Law in both business and in personal life. We have also moved almost all government provision of public goods into consumer owned or governed cooperatives which inherently regulate themselves. We have fixed the problem of monopolistic abuse of the consumer by large firms, we have removed most of the incentive towards crime through our aspirational new education system, we have changed the economic system such that it now invests in the Biosphere rather than consuming it, and we have eliminated Intellectual Property Law – in fact, from our studies of where the Legal system expends its resources, almost all of the current Legal system is no longer necessary under our proposals. Put quite frankly, the system looks after itself and the courts can return to pondering far weightier and more important issues which actually matter in the long run, much as they once used to in the late 19th and early 20th century.

16. Parliament should define Law, not its Implementation

Of course, there is a great need for specifics in Law: a general directive is by definition vague and incomplete and the courts would be overrun without very detailed and specific rules to arbitrate between grey areas. Furthermore, one major danger of keeping the Law fresh as we have proposed above is that any one government is given far too much power to completely transform current Law – such power corrupts very easily into tyranny, so we need a large and powerful counterweight.

We propose a very simple solution for this: let those with sufficient skill qualifications in Law define the detailed and specific *implementation* of legal directives issued by Parliament via a collaborative website much like Wikipedia. In case you think this impossible, this process happens every day in open source software development where volunteer programmers will implement a specification handed down to them by others. There is absolutely no reason why Law cannot be developed and maintained just like open source computer software – in fact, there is every reason that it *should* be operated in this way as it offers very significant economies of scale, allows any member of the public to participate, is a vastly improved way of implementing an upper house of Parliament (which can now be scrapped in lieu of this) and best of all, is completely open and transparent – something which most certainly cannot be said of the current process[28]. Because so many people are now familiar with Law and indeed bound into the actual process of its evolution and development, they offer a very powerful moderating influence on excessive government zeal.

People have the inalienable right to know and understand the rules by which they are governed. The current obese mess is so unknowable and arbitrary, even by its most expert practitioners, that it creates a Kafkaesque world where the innocent are guilty and the guilty are innocent. This serves no one's long term interests, and the whole legal system as it currently stands is grinding to a halt.

17. Regulate through Educate

We have alluded in our Education Proposals for skill based qualifications that something much bigger was coming as a replacement for legal regulation: we call it **freedom through qualification**. We make this 'Regulate Through Educate' proposal because we believe that every human being is borne into the chains of ignorance and incapability, and it is only through gaining experience, understanding and therefore wisdom can any person make a free choice.

For example, it is often said that a gun is a dangerous weapon – however, in truth it is only a *loaded* gun which is any more dangerous than a large rock. A person who does not know nor understand guns, most especially the difference in *potential consequences* of a gun, is robbed of their liberty by possessing a loaded gun because like a child, they are now constrained into using that loaded gun in order to discover its consequences. Many have observed that the citizens of Canada or Switzerland own more guns per person than the citizens of the United States, yet the rate of gun use against a human being in the US is dozens

---

[28] Indeed the current practice of Law is so opaque that very few members of the public have easy access to a Law Library. The only country of which we are aware that has attempted to place most of its current Law online is Britain. It was precisely because of this easy accessibility that the *Freeing Growth* books examine British Law rather than anyone else's.

of times more prevalent. How can this difference be explained? We hold that most gun possessing citizens are wise enough to never use their weapons against another human being, however to possess a thing whose consequences are not understood invites experimentation for the exact same reasons as scientists conducting experiments. This need to understand has been severely repressed in the Western world – this is why most murders involving guns are crimes of passion, usually by a man in a fit of rage. Not uncoincidentally, statistically men tend to experiment recklessly far more often than women.

We believe that freedom is extinguished by possessing access to something which one has neither earned nor deserves. One cannot possibly appreciate the gift bestowed upon life without earning one's living; much the same way we have squandered our material wealth on some of the most appalling trite. Most of us suffer severely from ingratitude under God's munificence – no wonder then that we live inside the Kingdom of God, but do not experience it.

We therefore propose that all activities which generate *potential* of negative consequences either to society or the individual which can be **easily** moderated shall be confined exclusively to those which possess the requisite skill qualifications.

How might this proposal be realised in practice? An awful lot of it is commonsense. For example, it is absolutely ludicrous that any adult can enter into a thirty-five year long mortgage contract involving hundreds of thousands of euro without an intimate understanding of compound interest. Because of how compounding works, a difference of one percent near the start of the contract can translate into tens of thousands of euro of extra cost (or indeed savings). If you would like to prevent a property bubble from ever happening again (much as caused the current credit crunch), a very good way is to require mortgage holders to possess a qualification in compound interest which must be renewed every five years. In particular, they should be adept at calculating net present value (NPV) under a series of scenarios such that they can optimise their repayment schedules according to changing market conditions – the banks of course will dislike this, however capital allocation efficiency would be greatly improved in an economy with consequent benefits for economic growth (far too much of potential consumer wealth is tied up in housing and in real estate in general – it should be out there growing the economy rather than as a method for the central bank to regulate disposable income. Remember, real estate wealth is effectively 'dead wealth' because it is tied up out of the economy – something the divorced money supply fixes). This particular form of Regulate through Educate is an example of 'negative liberty' whereby the system is structured to create freedom from oppression through ignorance by ensuring that only those who understand an economic contract may enter into it. It is equally an example of 'positive liberty' whereby the understanding instilled allows the consumer to take charge of their world, knowing that they know, and to fulfil their potential.

Another example of Regulate through Educate is that of unhealthy consumption e.g. psychoactive drugs (particularly alcohol which causes more harm than all the rest – including pharmaceuticals – combined), fatty and unbalanced heavily processed foods, excessive or unwise use of labour saving tools (especially transport) and so on, is not available to those not possessing the requisite skill qualifications. How can a person eat healthily if they have no understanding of what food is, how it is prepared nor what effects the consumption of different foods may have? Is it therefore not obvious why so many suffer from easily preventable diseases of malconsumption such as environmental diabetes, heart attacks and strokes? Imagine the effects upon economic growth if every person was as fit and healthy at the age of sixty as they were at the age of thirty?

Similarly, it is any wonder that there is drunken violence in almost every large town centre during the weekend, or that people continue to drink and drive? In fact most people with proper training can be quite safe drivers when moderately drunk, unfortunately a minority become so impaired even with small amounts of alcohol that they become such a liability that all drink driving has been banned for everyone. Yet because of the obvious holes in such logic – the fact that most people are perfectly capable of safe driving when drunk – drink driving continues even by those rendered incapacitated by it and who should never ever drive when drunk. Meanwhile, tens of thousands of lives continue to be snuffed out before their time with obvious consequences for economic growth.

Unlike some we most certainly do not advocate the absolute banning of any form of consumption at all: everyone should be free to do as they wish whether in public or in private. However, all consumption of anything must be done **responsibly** and with full understanding of the consequences of one's actions – otherwise one becomes imprisoned by unearned potential.

In the case of unhealthy consumption (for example hamburgers, psychoactive drugs etc), we propose that only those with the appropriate qualifications in nutrition for the hamburgers and in each psychoactive drug are permitted to purchase them. The purchaser may then give (but not sell, that requires an additional qualification as does manufacture) the proscribed item to others e.g. a qualified parent may buy a hamburger for their child, or a qualified friend may buy an Ecstasy tablet for another friend. For some foods/drugs where it is hard to immediately kill yourself, it should be permitted to manufacture your own at home for personal consumption without qualification (e.g. hamburgers, naturally grown marijuana), whereas others with a mild chance of blowing oneself up may require qualifications in order to purchase the manufacturing equipment (e.g. alcohol distillation, artificially grown marijuana). We anticipate different levels of qualification for different concentrations of active agent, so alcohol at less than 1.5% would require no qualification, below 10% level one, below 25% level two, below 40% level three, below 75% level four, below 100% level five and so on.

In the case of unhealthy behaviour (for example driving a car, riding a horse, unnecessary cosmetic surgery etc), we propose the institution of a system of automated restraint and regular checkups. For example, cars should simply not allow an unqualified driver to exceed the driving freedom permitted by their qualifications e.g. below 50kph level one, below 80kph level two, below 100kph level three, below 120kph level four, unlimited level five and so on. The car can know its driver through a fingerprint reader which turns on the ignition instead of a key – it then notifies the central content database which returns the driver's current qualifications and enables a randomised (and possibly compulsory – see next proposal) satellite tracking of the car during its journey to ensure that the car has not been tampered with. The car can also tell if a driver is impaired through drugs, alcohol or tiredness through analysis of driving pattern as compared to historical behaviour. This proposal may sound very 'Big Brother', however we do not anticipate a car whose functioning is arbitrarily imposed upon its drivers by others – in fact, we propose that the car's onboard computer system is open to third party modification such that any person can modify (most of) it as they see fit, thus choosing *how* their car regulates their driving but not *whether* it regulates their driving (this is quite possible given good computer software design). Traditionally this would open the temptation of spoofing the driver, however remember that we proposed properly implemented security protocols above which makes this possibility very difficult indeed unless you want to get caught (in other words, it is relatively easy for those who know how to spoof another driver, but the system will very rapidly identify your deception and ensure your capture and detainment). We also expect that it should be possible to obtain an 'elite' driving qualification which completely removes all driving restrictions, including behaviours which are currently illegal. Therefore, under our proposals, suitably qualified drivers would actually be more free on public roads than at any time since the early 20th century.

We believe that denial is one of the most important detractors from freedom that exists: most people would take preventative action to avoid heart disease, lung cancer or obesity if it hadn't just crept up upon them slowly. We therefore propose a system of regular checkups as part of gaining certain skill qualifications, so for example if one has the qualification for the consumption of tobacco, then one should undergo a regular health check such that the smoker is in full awareness of the direct and specific consequences to their own health. The same goes for fatty foods as much as for crack cocaine – the difference only arises in the degree of effect upon health.

Special Section restored in 2011

18. The Proposals for Old Age

In the heady days after World War II, there was a genuine sentiment that people would be looked after in their old age – they could be confident that a lifetime of work & thrift would be rewarded. Therefore, institutionalised healthcare & pensions were set up in every Western country and firms responded with lifetime career paths for most white collar workers. Meanwhile, mandatory pension contributions with generous tax breaks (really bribes) from the state ensured that vast amounts of money were funnelled into pension funds. Under the original Bretton Woods post-WW2 plan, the idea was that mass saving for people's retirements would provide the investment capital for massive industrial growth – and indeed, they were absolutely correct: Western economies grew rapidly after World War II, even ones not damaged by bombing. The US became the undisputed economic powerhouse of the world, but all Western nations also did well.

The most recently available figures (2009) put **invested** pension funds at 27% of global investment under active management, or about 45% of global annual GDP. That is the sum total amount of money which has been explicitly invested to provide for old age.

It is well known that approximately one third of net wealth in Western countries is under the control of the over sixty-fives. If however the value of the primary residence is removed, just **7.5%** of net wealth remains and this non-property wealth is very unevenly spread, with the bottom 40% of over-sixty fives having negligible wealth outside their main property and the top 20% holding most of the invested pension funds mentioned earlier. Put another way, 60-80% of retirees primarily rely on either the state or their former employer as their main source of income, with nothing other than the value of their primary residence to draw down upon if needed. And that is a LOT less provision for old age than you will typically read in government publications[29].

Here comes the problem: Firstly, the number of people born each year in most Western countries peaked no later than 1975, so there are fewer new taxpayers to replace retiring taxpayers as time goes on. Secondly, the temporary spike in people borne after the Second World War (the 'baby boomers'), around

---

[29] This is not to say that they aren't extremely aware of the truth. The problem has been that most public sector workers have better than average pension guarantees which are unfunded entitlements in excess to the 40% of retirees who rely exclusively on state pensions which are also unfunded. Put simply, we as a society have only been saving for retirement for just 20-30% of the population. And all of that was privately done.

0.5% of the working population, are going to retire before 2016 and because they were an abnormal spike, there is no one to replace them. I might add that most people are typically at their highest lifetime income level just as they approach retirement, so a substantial amount of tax income for governments is going to disappear (and indeed has already disappeared – these baby boomers started to retire from 2009, so some of the 2011 fiscal problems in Western governments is actually rapidly rising pension costs combined with dropping tax receipts).

This is bad, but isn't as bad as what is coming. The trouble with an abnormal spike in extra children is that they go on to have even more additional children themselves. The next rise in the rate of retirement begins from 2025 onwards (assuming a retirement age of 70), plateaus from 2035 and starts to fall from 2042, flattening out from 2047. The OECD thinks that the ratio of non-working to working age populations will go from 1:4 in 2005 to an average across the OECD of 1:2 by 2050, and to a frightening 1:1 in some OECD countries such as Italy, Spain or Japan[30]. In short, this ratio (called the '[old-age] dependency ratio' in the literature) is set to on average **double**.

You might not think that too bad on the face of things. You would be wrong for the following four reasons:

1. Unfunded entitlements based on unhistorical expectations, fraud and an awful lot of lies. The cupboard is bare!

2. Half of all healthcare already goes on the over sixties, squeezing out the young. Expect that to rise to two thirds!

3. A quarter of your taxes already goes on dying people. Expect your taxes to rise by a further **25%** to support a doubling of the dependency ratio!

4. Why would the young put up with this if the baby boomers didn't?

1. Unfunded entitlements based on unhistorical expectations, fraud and an awful lot of lies. The cupboard is bare!

Almost all Western governments, and most corporations have not invested sufficient funds to meet their pension obligations. This is called 'unfunded entitlements' in the literature, and in 2004 unfunded entitlements were 514% of GDP in the US and 434% of GDP in the EU25 for government promises *alone* (Gokhale, 2009). No one is exactly sure how unfunded company pensions are due to an acrimonious disagreement about the value of a thing called the

---

[30] Source: http://www.oecd.org/dataoecd/4/24/38148786.pdf.

'discount rate'. Put simply, many companies assume an average 8% p/a return for their pension fund investments, as do many governments, because this minimises how much of their present income they need to invest into the fund. They legitimise this by pointing out that the average rate of stock market growth between 1926 and 2005 was around 9%.

I find it absolutely fascinating how despite the recent falls in asset valuations, people **still** believe that stock markets and real estate are *always* the best store of value in the long term. Yet this belief is perhaps less ground in evidence than belief in eternal economic growth because, quite frankly, the past century was highly abnormal when seen from a historical perspective. The truth is that there were a series of one-off events starting from the recession of 1865 which, perhaps by chance, *just happen* to have led to abnormal rises in asset valuations faster than economic growth would otherwise have allowed.

While I agree that economic growth will always lead to investment growth, there is mounting evidence that the superior rate of stock market growth since 1926 is extremely unlikely to continue and furthermore, that real estate ought to be a LOT cheaper than it has been. Seeing as the entire of pension provision relies on outsize investment growth, and for the majority of pensioners their house is their only real store of wealth, please forgive me if I spend some time explaining in detail how the recent behaviour of asset valuations is highly unlikely to continue:

i. Thanks to fears of Communism, we experienced a widely distributed, rapid rise in wealth across the West, and one which is being slowly unwound now that the bogeyman of Communism has been exorcised and there is no longer any reason to distribute wealth widely. Witness the history 1820-1992 of inequality of income and life expectancy from Bourguigon and Morrison (2002) and note how income inequality dropped so precipitously 1920-1980 before starting to rise again:

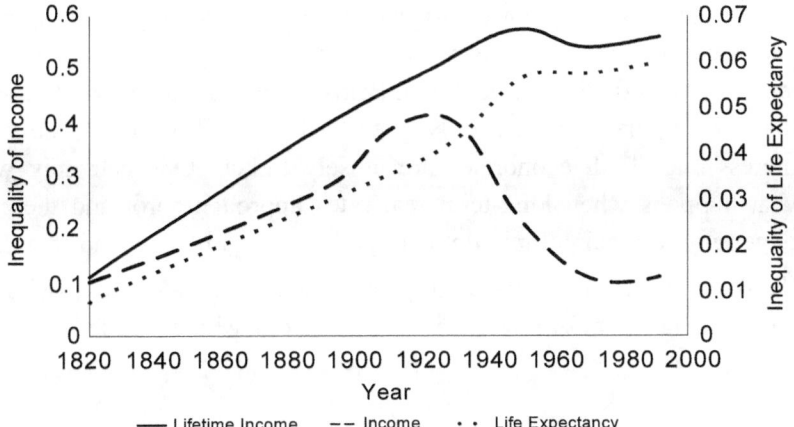

Even if income inequality is kept low, such an increase in distribution of wealth is a one-off occasion – it cannot be repeated again.

ii. We saw a departure from the gold standard, allowing a one-off large increase in liquidity much of which was used to pump up asset prices. One cannot depart from the gold standard a second time!

iii. Witness the history of Britain's real interest rates 1694-2010, chosen because they kept detailed records throughout the rise and decline of the British Empire. The real interest rate is the amount of financial reward earned by saving for later rather than borrowing or spending now:

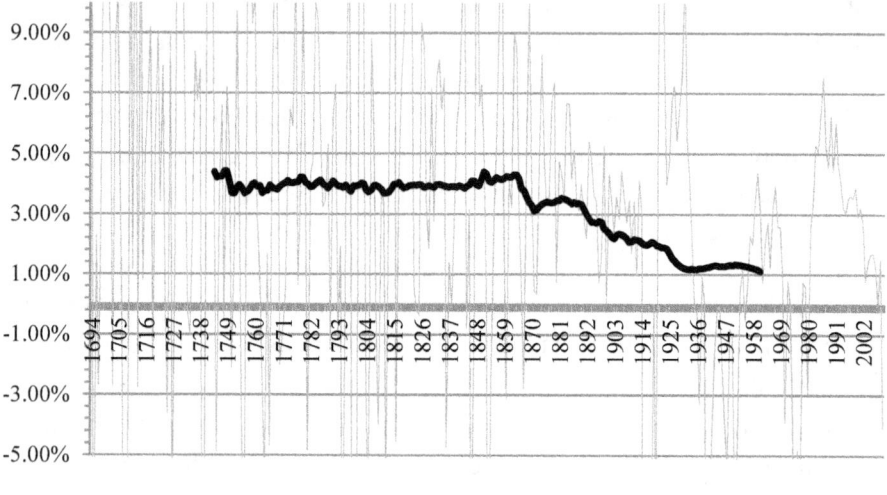

———— Real Interest Rate   ▬▬▬▬Hundred Year Rolling Average of Real Interest Rate

Note how – when averaged over a century – real interest rates stayed level centring on 3.98% for nearly the 175 years between 1694 and 1865; declined steadily until 1930, and have stayed level centring on 1.25% since until just after World War II when they began to decline again. Hence, the long-term reward for saving over borrowing is dropping, and continues to drop – and by the way, US real interest rates were approximately 0.75 correlated with British rates outside of war time during the past century (US data only goes back reliably to 1914), so for real interest rates both economies are closely linked. One can only wonder what happens when long-term real rates approach zero, and there is no longer any rational point in doing anything except borrow and spend.

iv. Thanks to these constantly falling real interest rates, a one-off switch from mass saving to mass borrowing has occurred which has led to total net debt (i.e. including personal debt) for most Western countries reaching between 300% and 400% of GDP[31] and rising banking reserve ratios, thanks to the financial collapse, will inhibit further lending for at least one generation (by which time we will likely have forgotten recently learned lessons about finance, and will no doubt repeat history yet again). This has had a curious effect on asset valuation: witness the house price index for the US when adjusted for inflation[32]:

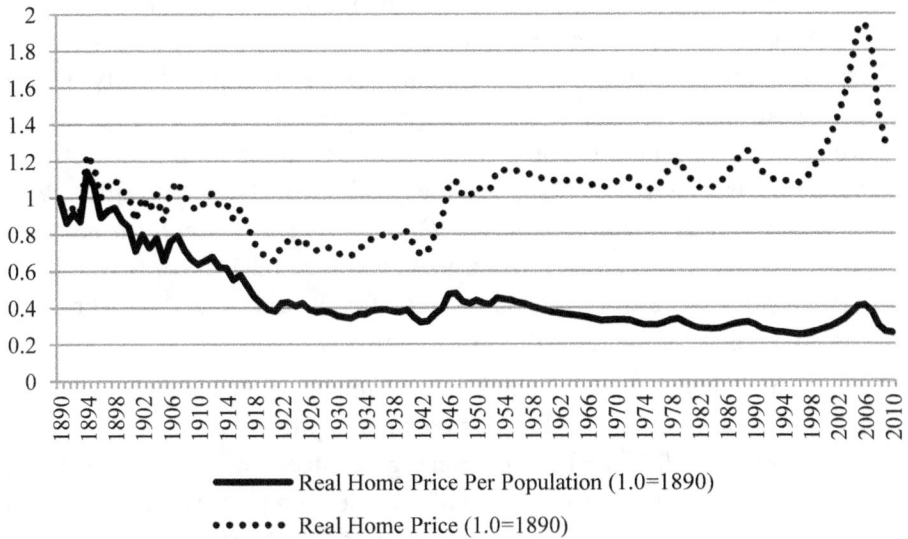

━━━ Real Home Price Per Population (1.0=1890)

•••••• Real Home Price (1.0=1890)

Despite what one might intuitively think, real house prices have remained remarkably steady in the US since 1890 (despite the hysteria about first time buyers/poor people/minorities not getting on ladders etc. causing ever larger infusions of government subsidies into unaccountable government sponsored entities [GSEs] like Fannie Mae), and when adjusted for the fact that more population means more demand for housing one finds a *fall* in real housing cost per capita to about **one quarter** of the 1890 cost per capita.

This is surprising, but probably not for the reasons you are thinking. It is surprising because *the drop in real housing cost per capita is so small* when so many other things fell far more substantially in price during the same time period. For example, between 1890 and 2010 real US GDP per

---

[31] Source: *The Economist*, (2010-Jun), 'Special report: Debt'.

[32] Source: Tables from *Irrational Exuberance* by Robert Shiller at http://www.econ.yale.edu/~shiller/data/Fig2-1.xls.

capita rose tenfold; real income per capita rose eightfold[33] and productivity per employee 1890-2006 in the US rose sevenfold (Cette, Kocoglu, & Mairesse, 2010), so really the drop in the real housing cost per capita is about half what it ought to be. One cannot help but wonder whether the fourfold substitution of capital for labour between 1900 and 2000 (Ayres & Warr, 2006) is coincidental or covariant with the fall in real housing cost per capita, but I digress.

Note the drop in real house prices (dotted line) of **one third** between 1890 and 1930, and which when adjusted per capita (solid line) is almost a straight line. Before 1934, a typical mortgage required fifty percent collateral and was usually between five and seven years long. In 1934 Roosevelt brought in thirty year long mortgages with government assuming the additional risk, but few availed of them until after World War II when *veterans were given the entitlement to obtain a mortgage without collateral* (i.e. the government guaranteed the loan). Now note the sudden 50% spike in real house prices after World War II to where they remained, in inflation-adjusted terms, until 1997.

Here is my theory – and I will admit it is not supported by the literature: I think that real housing cost per capita would have dropped far *lower* than fourfold had government guaranteed mortgages never been introduced to approximately a sevenfold reduction (as it would make sense that the value of housing is surely tied strongly to productivity). I think that the effect of such mass borrowing was to **drive up** the price of housing to the disproportionate financial benefit of those who did the lending and building to the financial loss of those who got a house earlier than they otherwise would[34]. And I think that considering how high the net debt ratio has become, and how low the real interest rate has fallen, that this is yet another bubble that is going to pop in the next twenty years. Given how many trillions of dollars are wrapped up in stock market listed

---

[33] Source: The extremely useful website http://www.measuringworth.com/.

[34] Given the large, sustained rise in take home pay after the war, almost every veteran after World War II would have been able to afford a home anyway. They just had to wait a few years, but in exchange would have saved several years worth of annual income each. More importantly, in my opinion *all* house prices would then be 75% lower in 2010 as the self-reinforcing inflating effects of a competitive race for more borrowing would have been avoided, which in turn means that there would have been **no sub-prime collapse**, young people could much more easily buy homes, which in turn leads to a much higher net savings rate across society which in turn means that the West wouldn't be paying so much interest on the loans lent to us by developing nations. In short, the West would be in a *far* better state than the present. And all for waiting a few extra years for a house just after World War II!

GSEs, that means falling asset valuations across the board, so think of how an additional 2007 recession would affect pension funds and house prices and you're getting to where I think it still has yet to go.

Thankfully, my opinion that asset valuations have further to drop is not completely unsupported by the literature. So unusual was the demography of the past century that the Federal Reserve, among many others, thinks that asset prices are likely to start trending downwards as new retirees start drawing down their pensions and thus pulling money out of the bubble investment system (Liu & Spiegel, 2011), reducing US stock market valuations by 14% before 2020. A statistical cross-country-comparative analysis in a paper by an international bank (Takáts, 2010) suggested that a 1% rise in GDP per person and a 1% rise in the total population each correspond to around a 1% rise in real house prices. Conversely, a 1% increase in the old-age dependency ratio correlates with a 0.66% drop in real house prices. Japan, whose dependency ratio rose earliest, has been in stagnation since the 1990s – whether this is indeed due to a rising dependency ratio, or more a cultural problem, we shall shortly find out as our own dependency ratio is rising rapidly.

Whatever the case, an 8% discount rate for pension fund investment is clearly far, far too high. So what would be a better discount rate? Historical growth in dividends – which one would assume is the most reliable, if typically understated[35], measure of value – between 1874 and 2004 was just 1.7%, and even during the boom years since 1980 it has been just 2.6%. Even world GDP grew by just 4% p/a since 1950, and empirical economic studies show that **investment growth in aggregate can never exceed GDP growth minus two percent** (Bernstein & Arnott, 2003). On this basis a discount rate of 2% below GDP growth would be prudent i.e. between 2% and 3%, not 8%. And to give you an idea of why a 5% shortfall is so important, a shortfall of 5% p/a, after thirty years, leaves a pension fund at just **23%** of what is needed to fully meet its obligations.

Finally, in the past twenty years there has been a very large rise in pension compensation for senior management where US$20m-US$100m pensions *per job position* are granted. This is funded from the general employee pension fund, but unlike for normal workers the entitlements for senior management are almost never explicitly provided for at the time of employment i.e. they are unfunded obligations, just like those unfunded pensions promised by governments. Hence, we are seeing a slow unfunding of previously funded

---

[35] It is typically understated because a firm may choose to use profits to grow rather than pay investors.

entitlements to the benefit of senior management and at the expense of everyone else. Personally I would call this fraud, but unfortunately it is quite legal in most (but not all) Western countries.

What all this means, in aggregate, is that most companies will not pay out the full value of pensions when the time comes, or if they do it will be at a below subsistence level. That implies that these 'private' pensioners will turn to the state instead, so the young taxpayer is ultimately on the hook for all this. This means that the unfunded entitlements that we know about promised by governments are in fact just the tip of the iceberg, and the rainy day fund is quite literally empty.

2. Half of all healthcare already goes on the over sixties, squeezing out the young. Expect that to rise to two thirds!

If you look into dependency on healthcare, you will find that **right now** the over sixties consume 55-60% of all healthcare expenditure in the West for the simple reason that older people fall ill more frequently and take longer to recover. As more people retire, that share is set to rise by probably around a half, and overall healthcare expenditure as a proportion of the economy will surely increase. That might not matter too much in European countries where healthcare costs are reasonable due to centrally enforced cost control, but for the US where they have been spiralling ever upwards for decades now it is another unsustainable bubble.

3. A quarter of your taxes already goes on dying people. Expect your taxes to rise by a further 25% to support a doubling of the dependency ratio!

If you add together present (2008) government spending on healthcare and pensions, you will find that around 10% of GDP **already** goes on the over-65s just from the government alone. Given typical taxation rates in Western countries, that means between 20-30% of present government spending is already on the old, or put another way, **a quarter of your taxes already goes on dying people**.

Doubling the number of people dependent on taxpayers suggests that the amount spent to support them will double. That implies a rise in average taxation levels of about 25-30%. Given that the total tax revenues as a percentage of GDP (called the 'tax burden' in the literature) in the West is generally between 30% (US) and 50% (Sweden), that implies a rise of that taxation to at least half of GDP and more likely 60% of GDP in countries which have least invested for their future such as the US. To put that in perspective, very few Western countries have ever exceeded a 50% total tax burden for any length of time, including wartime – and only Denmark has ever exceeded 60%. Even in 'high tax' Europe[36], the average total tax revenues as a percentage of GDP was just 35% in the early 1970s, rising to 38% in the late 1970s, and plateauing at 41% throughout the 1980s and 1990s before dropping back to under 40% during the 2000s[37].

4. Why would the young put up with this if the baby boomers didn't?

Given how for the present younger generation there will always be more older people than them above them, why would the typical young person of today ever believe that they will retire before they are too sick to work? Therefore why would they continue to prop up the unsustainable pension bubble, especially in the face of declining asset valuations where every home owner is trapped in negative equity and every pension fund stagnates or declines in value over time?

The last point matters much more than you might think. Most Western countries haven't raised income taxes by much in the past ten years because the politicians think it will prevent their election. However, the rate of mandatory pension contributions has been creeping upwards from a typical rate of around 5% in the 1990s, to around 10% in the 2000s and is on course to average 15% in the 2010s. These increases are to date politically acceptable as taxpayers think that the extra money taken from them is stored somewhere by government in a kind of bank account, and indeed official government statistics don't include mandatory pension contributions when calculating tax burdens. Unfortunately, the truth is that almost all Western countries simply treat most or all of these contributions as general taxation. This stealth rise in income tax is therefore only politically acceptable *so long as people continue to believe they will receive it back as a pension on retirement*. If that belief should fray e.g. if the date of retirement is set too high, or the payment reduced to too low, mandatory pension contributions will be seen for what they are: **income tax by another name**.

In short, anyone rational or sensible would have very serious concerns about the sustainability of the present system, and the only Western country that I

---

[36] Europe isn't actually that high tax overall when compared to other countries – it merely taxes individuals much more heavily than companies e.g. Value Added Tax (VAT) adds 15-25% to all purchases by individuals but 0% to all purchases by companies, and income tax rates for individuals can be as much as twice corporation tax rates for companies. This is done because empirical studies have shown this allocation of taxation to be the least deleterious from an economic perspective.

[37]   Source: http://epp.eurostat.ec.europa.eu/cache/ITY_OFFPUB/KS-DU-07-001/EN/KS-DU-07-001-EN.PDF.

know of with a semi-sane pension system is Australia and even that suffers from substantial unfunded entitlements. I think the whole old age support edifice is going to snap, and snap sooner rather than later.

Is retirement moral?

Putting aside the fact that the present arrangement is completely unsustainable financially, one **must** ask the question: is it *moral* to direct 20% of GDP and more than two thirds of healthcare expenditure at supporting dying people? These are people at the end of their lives, and they will no doubt expend most of their total retirement income on healthcare propping them up at huge expense for just a few extra years. While they have experience valuable to society, the value of that experience is not the same as in the past in this increasingly technological world, and one can make a reasonable argument that for many types of job, anyone over the age of fifty is probably inhibiting growth and that role would be better filled by someone younger – unless that older worker is being constantly retrained in how to best use new technologies, which presently, they typically are not because it is cheaper in many Western countries for employers to replace talent than maintain talent[38].

Moreover, there is a major problem of *moral hazard* here. What is happening is that government and many corporations **lied** and **continue to lie** to workers about the extent for which their pensions have been provided. That is real unfortunate for the majority who have been screwed out of a comfortable retirement, but the fault here lies with those who told the lies and those who believed and believe them and didn't hold the counterparty to their end of the agreement. The people who lied should, in my opinion, be ferreted out, prosecuted and thrown into prison for financial fraud on a massive scale. However, why should younger taxpayers be required to bail out the mistakes of their forefathers?

In short, I don't think that they should. I don't think that anyone looking at it from a moral viewpoint can argue that they should. I also think it is too easy for the children to shove the costs and responsibilities of looking after their parents onto society. And I think it is too easy for grandparents to abrogate their moral

---

[38] Much ink is spilled over the 'structural unemployment' problem in Europe and how it is too costly to hire and fire employees. This over-simplifies the problem: the very high costs to hire and fire employees was intended to encourage employers to invest in their employees rather than externalise their support onto society by 'refreshing' a position with a younger, more recently educated (and cheaper) candidate e.g. in Spain, it is very common for employers to regularly send their older employees on training programmes, whereas in the United States it is seen as the *employee's* responsibility to place themselves on training programmes in order to maintain their attractiveness to the employer.

duty to teach their experience to their grandchildren and serve the community in the ways that only the experienced can.

I also don't think it wise to direct a large proportion of the income generated by our society into the healthcare system which misallocates healthcare towards supporting the dying. The healthcare system ought to be about supporting those who incur life events or misfortune, the failure of which to alleviate would otherwise prevent them contributing to society in the future. This is not to say that anyone no longer able to contribute should be shoved into a death camp – compassion is after all is the mark of the civilised. But let's be reasonable here: directing **one fifth** of economic output into supporting the dying is **stupid**. We have an obligation to look after the weak and unfortunate in our society – indeed, all these proposals in aggregate transform the problem of marginalisation and poverty greatly for the better. So let us see how I would suggest these proposals ought to be applied to the aged:

What to do about the aged

You will remember, I am sure, how sin taxation replaces all taxation apart from the depreciation tax which is the only general tax. Almost all services presently provided by the government are now provided by consumer governed cooperatives, and things like hospitals are entirely governed by the local population which makes use of them. Any corporation which becomes large enough can be converted into a consumer governed cooperative through a vote of its customers, and that wouldn't cause shareholders to yank their investment thanks to the new risk differentiated shareholding structure proposed.

Remember also how everyone now spends half their time in education taking skill modules of understanding, which when successfully passed give them a specific freedom until the module expires through depreciation of their ϵ_a value and a refresher module must be regularly taken to reacquire the right to that freedom. And remember that people are paid when they pass these modules, with the amount of pay rising as the module of demonstrated skill understanding becomes more advanced.

The solution for retirement therefore becomes very clear. Being unemployed means you get no income from society whatsoever, so if you cannot find a job then your only recourse is to improve oneself through study. I see no difficulty that the same cannot apply to the old, because there is no longer any artificial distinction between those who do not work because they are 'old' and those who do not work for any other reason. In fact, *there is no retirement* unless you personally save up for one yourself by directing your income into a retirement fund – we no longer live in a world where heavy physical labour exhausts the body, so there is no longer a need to assume that the old need looking after in reward for a lifetime of heavy labour. In the 2008 book, but not in the relevant section above, I proposed that all bank accounts default[39] to saving twenty-five percent of any $€_r$ money arriving into them into a savings account denoted in $€_a$ (all monies earned from obtaining education modules are denoted entirely in $€_a$ anyway). If a person withdraws money from that $€_a$ savings account for the purposes of non-investment expenditure, they incur the $€_a$ to $€_r$ sin tax conversion spread set by the central bank which would penalise them for doing so. I think that would be a pretty strong incentive to save throughout your lifetime.

In fact, such now would be the propensity to save, I would propose that inheritance law is substantially changed. Where at the moment it defaults to your nearest next of kin upon your death, I would propose that it ought to default to the *children* of your nearest next of kin. And instead of paying out on death, it ought to start being transferred incrementally at a rate determined by the central bank from either the moment that the first grandchild is born, or the person reaches ten years before the average age of death for their demographic. For example, the central bank might set a rate of transfer of 5% p/a though they would change it according to economic conditions, with the main criteria being to ensure that no sector of the economy becomes primarily directed towards servicing the dying (the past) over servicing the young (the future).

This particular proposal of before death inheritance seems to get a lot of people very upset. I don't know why – I am speaking of the *default* rules of inheritance. A person can, if they choose, write a will setting different rules directing the drawdown of their accumulated wealth to any destination they choose. However, the drawdown itself would be unavoidable – people may choose where it goes, and choose for it to happen earlier than ten years before the average age of death for their demographic, but they cannot choose that it does not happen.

And why not one might ask? Very simple: if people are permitted to retain their wealth as they approach old age, they will be tempted to expend it on expensive and wasteful measures to prolong their life which over-resources and corrupts the medical industry away from serving the future of society rather than serving the dying. People die – that is unavoidable. Instead of choosing a

---

[39] The default savings rate per account can be changed to zero or any other value, but if below twenty-five percent it will automatically start rising such that it returns to twenty-five percent after five years – unless reset to a lower value in the meantime.

poor quality but longer life, people should accept the consequences of any poor choices that they made which have led to poor health later on in life instead of irresponsibly frittering away resources on their own selfish and immoral desire to not accept the reality than their time is coming to an end. Of course, with the extensive sin taxation, and given that one cannot buy unhealthy foods or engage in unhealthy behaviours without having the skill module to enable the freedoms to do so, and of course the requirement to work or study until one is no longer physically or mentally able to do so, I would doubt that most old people will experience the mental and physical deterioration so omnipresent in today's senior citizens. In fact, I see no reason why the average age of death should not exceed one hundred years and that the quality of life up until that point ought to be excellent for most folk.

And why transfer the wealth to those just barely into adulthood? Because *they're the ones who need it*. Look around at today's society: up to the age of twenty-one, each new child costs about the same as a house on average. Young couples are typically in debt to between fifteen and twenty times the average take-home pay. That constrains how well the children can be raised, much to the detriment of all society when taken in aggregate. Remember how children learn half of what they will ever know by the age of seven? Put plainly, raising children and getting it right is hard enough without being hobbled by debt. This measure also ensures a greater incentive to connect grandparents with their grandchildren whilst keeping the incentive to save and accumulate wealth during your life. Best of all, instead of saving out of self*ish*ness, one now saves out of self*less*ness for those who will inherit the Earth you left them.

This brings us onto what to do with people when they do become too old or ill to work or study. The solution here is also easy: children have a moral obligation to look after their parents. If they fail to look after their parents, they will be sin taxed appropriately in order to provide for their parents – and I am sure given the cost, they will find a way to make it happen except where relations are so rancorous that they would prefer the sin tax. For those people without living relatives, the aforementioned automatic drawdown of their accumulated wealth should suffice for their care and if that should become exhausted, the (typically minimal given how few use it) subscriptions paid by everyone to their local consumer governed old age home cooperative should cover them for the few years remaining after becoming too old or ill to work or study.

As for those who from an early age suffer from extreme dementia, madness or other severely debilitating illnesses which are not of their own causing[40], these fall under the aegis of the local consumer governed health cooperative. There will always be a small percentage of people who are simply misfortunate, and each locality should choose to what level it will provide for such people. Do remember that the level of subscriptions taken from everyone are set by a vote of only those who have the requisite educational skill qualification to do so, and as part of that educational module I would think it prudent that the student experiences a few days in such hospices such that they intimately know what under-resourcing will do.

Lastly, there is the final point of what to do about pension funds. Right now they are obligated by law to maximise returns, and therefore force the firms they invest in to asset strip themselves, rape the biosphere and mistreat and overwork the children of the very people whose pension fund it is. This is stupid, and it causes much damage in the world. It would be extremely easy to rewrite the present 'value maximisation at all costs' requirement to a simple 'maximise benefit to the planet, then society, whilst maintaining a profit' requirement (indeed, I would argue that all firms and corporations ought to have their mandate similarly changed by legislative fiat). This single change could be done without anything else in this Manifesto – it's not rocket science, yet for some daft reason we don't mentally link how our pension funds work with how our corporations treat the planet. *Change the investment & allocation system, change the world.*

---

[40] Remember that the number of people able to intentionally make themselves ill would be highly limited because one must earn and retain the qualification to buy or create anything dangerous, and sin taxation starts to rise rapidly if one keeps doing or failing to do an activity which affects their health. For this small number remaining, one must consider whether they are mentally ill, or criminal, or virtuous and an example to be punished or extolled. For example, a person may deliberately give themselves a fatal illness in order to test a controversial cure upon themselves – this would be a highly laudable act, and society owes a great debt to anyone who sacrifices themselves in such a way for the greater good, and therefore such a person should be made as comfortable as possible under public funds.

The TBTI Proposal

19. Free the Information, Free the Growth!

So far, all our proposals have been relatively small and contained – despite their apparent breadth of scope, they are nothing like as broad as this last and final proposal: the 'Too Big To Imagine' proposal for the ultimate increase in sustainable growth. We must state clearly for the record that we ourselves are uncomfortable with this proposal, we find its implications distasteful and to be honest, we find it hard to conceive of a world in which it were the case.

Nevertheless, we find our hand forced by a series of inevitabilities. All growth – whether technological, biological, whatever – invariably follows a thing called a *logistic curve* which looks like an elongated 'S':

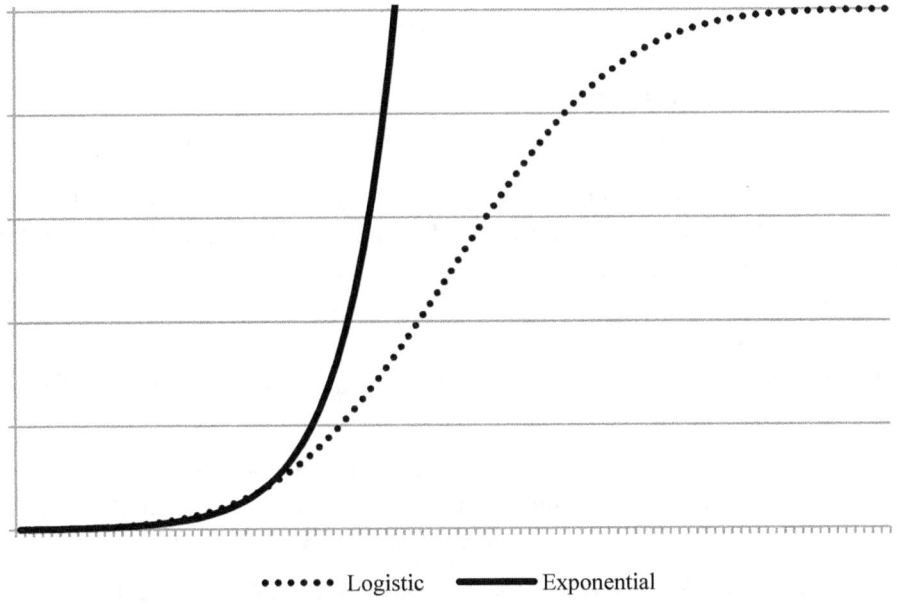

•••••• Logistic   ━━━━━ Exponential

In the early part of a logistic curve, growth appears exponential due to the compounding of the growth of earlier growth: just like our stock markets, GDP, semiconductor density (i.e. Moore's Law) and so on. However, eventually hard (usually physical) constraints begin to take effect which reduces growth to linear, and eventually to exponential decline before growth stops dead. If you know and understand this logistic progression, one realises that nobody can predict when exponential growth turns linear (i.e. when exponential growth stops), but once it has turned linear you can most certainly predict to a reasonable degree of accuracy when growth will stop by simply extrapolating the curve. For example, if we take computer storage technology[41]:

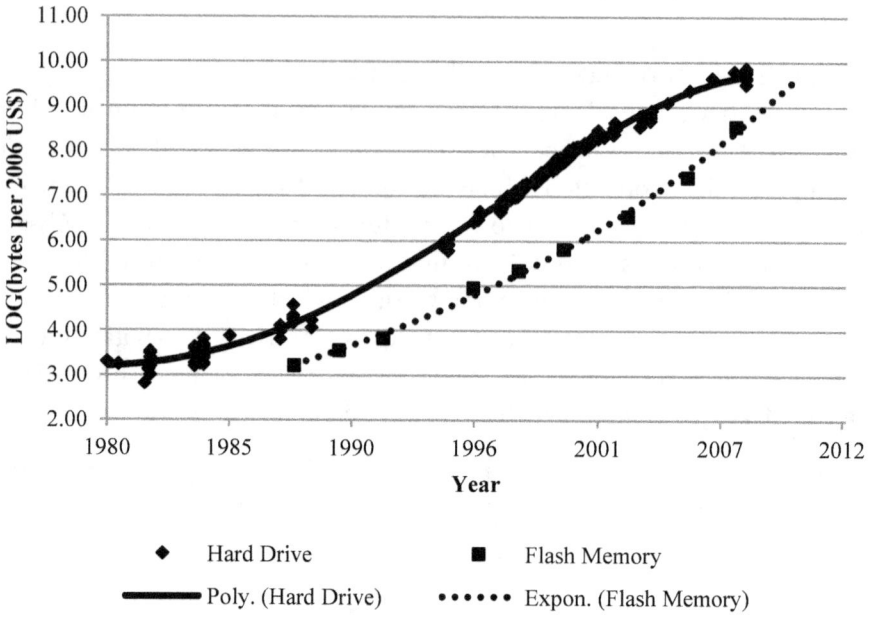

As is very obvious from this graph, computer hard drive technology has already begun its period of exponential decline. From extrapolating this graph, one can predict that flash memory storage will overtake as value leader around 2010, whereupon spinning magnetic computer storage will cease to be commonly used.

If you repeat this kind of analysis across human civilisation, one finds a most disturbing pattern:

1. The system knows your current geographical location to within a few metres thanks to the unique radio tag almost every single Western person carries with them (it is better known as the mobile phone)[42].

2. The system knows your daily habits, patterns and movements. It knows what you like to buy through tracking your plastic and loyalty cards, it can track the licence plate of your car, it knows the balances of all your bank accounts through the centralised credit checking system [43]. Increasingly it even knows where you walk inside a shopping mall, how

---

[41] Sources: for hard drive data, see http://www.littletechshoppe.com/ns1625/winchest.html. For flash memory data, we composited figures for Intel's flash memory technology website.

[42] Example: http://www.followus.co.uk/

[43] Example: http://www.annualcreditreport.co.uk/

long you stay at which shelf[44] and of course it knows who you regularly contact by phone or text message.

3. The system can accurately predict your voting intentions, the newspapers you read, your internal doubts, insecurities and biases, your hobbies and interests – the detail of the Experian marketing database[45] alone would shock many average people. Anyone can purchase access to these marketing databases for a modest fee.

4. The system knows and tracks everything you ever search for on the internet[46], it knows which sites you visit, it knows which kind of pornography you may like, it knows the content of every email you have ever sent or received and moreover, it is legally required to keep at least a six month or longer history of all these. If you're a member of Facebook or Bebo, its knowledge of you is even more detailed, including detailed friendship relations and tracking of these over time through analysis of uploaded photographs and messaging.

5. Thanks to exponential improvements in real-time satellite tracking technology, very soon indeed we can track any arbitrary moving object wherever it goes in the world including when it is cloudy or at night. Currently there is an affordable processing power limit which keeps the maximum item count in the tens of thousands, however advances in stream processing technology[47] will affordably raise this to millions in the next two years. **By 2012 there is no reason why every Western citizen cannot be individually tracked in real-time**.

It is only a matter of time before these bits of real-time information are tied together such that mobile phone tracking can be combined with satellite tracking and CCTV footage tracking. Even if government does not invest in this combination, private industry most certainly will because it is very useful in helping them to sell you things that you don't need and given our current economic state, government will not stop them trying to stimulate demand in any way that they can.

The traditional response is to pass even more regulation to try and control this technological inevitability. Such regulation is useless because it is

---

[44] Example: http://www.pathintelligence.com/

[45] Example: http://www.experian.co.uk/

[46] Example: http://www.google.com/trends/

[47] This specifically refers to the Intel 'Larrabee' processor (and its descendants) which is due early 2010. It significantly steepens the exponential incline of improvement in computer processing power.

impossible to enforce in practice: even if you send inspectors around to physically check people, it is extremely easy to hide one's activities. Furthermore, there is an extremely easy way of circumventing such laws: simply outsource its processing into a less regulated country via a 'consultant' who handles the dirty deeds for you, and whom can be scapegoated should anyone get caught (an identical technique is used by the West to outsource torture).

We believe that all these attempts to control information are doomed to failure in the long run. We believe that giving one set of people privileged access to such personal information creates an unstoppable incentive for moral corruption and **will** lead to the downfall of society, because ultimately no one can sufficiently watch the watchers.

Furthermore, we proposed the educational, corporate, governmental and legal reforms which we have because our modelling shows that the rate of growth increases as we reduce the disparity of information asymmetries i.e. as we reduce the lag in the dissemination of understanding, the more rapidly that most groups of people come to an understanding of a new concept or idea, and therefore the more rapidly economic growth occurs. We selectively applied this piecemeal to certain industries or certain sectors, but in truth there is no good reason why what is good for the goose is also good for the gander, and therefore to take the theory to its logical conclusion by extending it to its maximum everywhere.

It is extremely hard to describe such a world. Everyone can watch everyone else at all times equally. Everyone can rummage around everyone else's email, bank accounts, past and present phone calls, watch them having sex in the privacy of their own houses, track their movements across the globe and of course inspect every detailed aspect of their lives both at work and at home. Because everyone also knows who is watching them, we think that out of courtesy privacy will remain intact for all but celebrities (but then celebrities already have a fairly identical problem today). Bosses can watch employees, employees can watch bosses, wives and husbands can watch one another, as can children and parents, as can courts and criminals ... as the list grows longer, the harder it becomes to imagine the likely effects on society, culture, the individual, rates of crime or the gap in wealth or indeed anything else. Nevertheless, the *Freeing Growth* books make as good an attempt as any, and **such a proposal effectively makes lying and blackmail completely obsolete for the first time in human history**.

We don't like this proposal: even though our models show not just exponential growth, but hyperbolic growth which is when the growth of growth is exponential – such rapid growth would tear apart a society and culture which wasn't fully prepared for it. But we see it as the least worst choice given the alternatives of inevitably guaranteeing a tyranny as an elite few abuse their privileged information to exploit and bully the masses, or deliberately retrograding technological progress by simply destroying these advances outright. We also can see that a very great deal of good could come out of it: such a world is as close to the universal light (information) and truth of the Kingdom of God as described by His Prophets (any religion) as our minds can perceive, so hence this proposal appears to definitely be enacting the wisdom of the ancients.

What we are absolutely certain of is that present society is simply not ready for the widespread implementation of this proposal – it's too disruptive to traditional modes of Western human behaviour (which is primarily one of abusing all we behold while in a state of profound denial). The day it becomes imaginable to more than a few is the day it will become likely, and it could be implemented on an individual opt-out basis so long as the possibility for one person to impersonate another is permanently eliminated. We are absolutely, one hundred percent sure that this proposal is the inevitable destiny of human civilisation at some point because ALL trends in technological progress point in an identical direction. Put quite frankly, we think this inevitability is inescapable, and these proposals have been designed as the first stepping stone between now and then.

Sadly, we cannot see this 'Too Big To Imagine' proposal being even considered as viable until at least one tyranny, as we have predicted here, has demonstrated through horrific example why it is the only viable way forward. We too often assume that we are more civilised than our forefathers – in truth, we have only become much better at hiding the truth of our reality from ourselves. When push comes to shove, Western civilisation will redisplay the savagery and ruthlessness which propelled it to the top of the world. We only hope that once our predictions come true, we will be wise enough to forever remove the incentives towards moral corruption which asymmetries of power and information always provoke.

CHAPTER 4

Concluding Remarks

We believe that what we have proposed is not just one way of averting the imminent collapse of human civilisation, but will produce a world which is such an improvement upon what came before that we are actually proposing a quantum leap in the quality of life. We can do an awful lot more with less if we are smarter in how we do things.

Much of the detail of that quality and process has been left out of this Manifesto for reasons of space and the wish to not overwhelm the reader any more than necessary. What is not so obvious is how our proposals make these reforms *optional* in the sense that each country or region can enact them in whole or in part without disturbing trade and doing business in general. Unlike our predecessor *The Communist Manifesto*, we neither foresee nor wish for a violent revolution: violent revolutions are bad for everyone except arms manufacturers. We would much prefer a slow, steady evolution over time with ample time for reflection. After all, we may well have made a grave and catastrophic mistake (though we are quite sure that we have not!).

If you would like to know more, then choose your poison: this Manifesto has a Bibliography, the websites on the cover page have plenty of additional information, and of course we would strongly encourage you to invest in one or more of the *Freeing Growth* books (preferably via http://www.freeinggrowth.org/buy/ as this donates the commission from Amazon to the Freeing Growth charity). This Manifesto, and indeed the Books, shall be kept maintained and up-to-date and therefore shall be periodically rereleased as (hopefully) improved editions over time.

Lastly, thank YOU for reading this Manifesto! We hope that you enjoyed it! If you liked it, feel free to pass on as many copies to others as you wish (you can download copies from http://www.neocapitalism.org/ or purchase printed copies from the same).

The Assumptions

In order to present the predictions and proposals of this Manifesto, a great many assumptions had to be taken as given. Some have accused us of a negative and impoverished view of what it is to be a human being, and many have felt that our predictions of the future are unnecessarily pessimistic.

Most of the more contentious assumptions are explained at length in the books – despite this, most contemporary people will still disagree anyway because ultimately they are articles of reasoned *faith* and therefore are not strictly empirically required. It is not the purpose of this document to debate the following assumptions, but we do list as many of them as we can for completeness.

1. There will be plenty of energy available to human civilisation in the near future

We have assumed that there will be no *absolute* energy shortage at any stage in the next century which is a big assumption to make, but we feel a reasonable one. The coming 'energy crunch' is not one of scarcity of energy, but rather one of scarcity of *transportable* energy. Fossil hydrocarbons, in the form which power our transport at normal atmospheric temperatures and pressures, yield around 45-55MJ/kg which is about as energetically dense a practical energy transport known to our science. Hydrogen fuel[48] can easily treble that energy

---

[48] We have strong reservations with the widespread use of hydrogen gas as fuel. Firstly, its generation is not as energy efficient as organic energy transports nor ever can be no matter what technological improvements we make, so it is simply a poor technical solution. Secondly, there will be leakage of hydrogen gas into the atmosphere whereupon, it being extremely light, it shall float off into space and therefore permanently deprive the biosphere of water while leaving an unnatural excess of highly toxic oxygen. Put simply, hydrogen fuel is neither long-term sustainable nor does it integrate easily into natural biosphere carbon-based energy cycles – we should be sensible and not lock ourselves into this technology.

density, but even at seven hundred times atmospheric pressure it still only transports one sixth of the energy for the same volume as gasoline. Our best available reasonably priced batteries currently carry one twentieth the energy density and at thirty times the volume. Even if both hydrogen and battery technologies see multiple doublings of improvement, it is not hard to imagine the profundity of the probable consequences when the cheap hydrocarbons run out. Transport technology will be slower, heavier and much more expensive.

We do not however believe that this means the end of the personal automobile, but we do believe that future personal transport will not travel very far nor fast – though still better than a horse. Air travel shall become exclusive to the very wealthy and almost all heavy goods (e.g. food) shall become transported by sea and canal which significantly lengthens transport time and means that unseasonal foods shall become the privilege of the wealthy. Road haulage as we have known it shall simply vanish except where canals cannot be built.

Unless there is a very radical and unexpected technological improvement, these changes cannot be avoided nor changed – they are as inevitable as the sun rising each morning. However, we have assumed that electrical energy shall remain plentiful on the basis that if so incentivised, a great deal of non-fossil electricity generation capacity could be constructed relatively quickly. We would **strongly** point out that direct current (DC) transfers are far more efficient and useful than alternating current (AC) now that we have the transistor switching technology which the pioneers of electricity did not – switching to DC could **halve** the number of nuclear power stations we shall have to build which therefore halves the amount of nuclear waste produced. We also recognise that there are improved nuclear fission designs which can produce a fifth of the nuclear waste or better (though with a much increased radioactivity and toxicity), and furthermore that some new nuclear power stations will be needed for the times when Nature is not blowing much wind around.

We also very strongly advocate the holistic locating of sun-collecting steam turbine power stations in the south of the EU and US which pump power via high-tension DC electrical cables to the more overcast north where tidal and wave power is not practical or available. Unlike some, we view geothermal as a *store* of energy rather than a source: heavily tapping geothermal will produce devastating earthquakes in some parts of the world and may destabilise the Earth's protective magnetic shield, whereas pumping energy in during the summer and out during the winter is a far safer and more sustainable approach in the long-term. We need to accept that the 'free' energy lunch we have gorged ourselves upon is unhealthy, and that simply substituting 'free' geothermal for hydrocarbons will not help us – the only truly long-term sustainable energy source is the Sun. Geothermal can act as a battery, but it is not inexhaustible.

To conclude, we do not anticipate an energy shortage – we have more than plenty of affordable options. We do however predict a severe hydrocarbon crunch which means the end of cheap transport and cheap artificial nitrogen fixation (which relies heavily on natural gas) with the concomitant severe effects upon food availability and speed of transport. In particular, we foresee as a result an *increase* in the use of the internet and computer information technologies in order to 'virtually travel' where one physically no longer can. This is because most of the energy inputs into operating computer technology can be successfully moved from fossil to electrical, and besides computer technology has been the main driver of economic growth in the West from the 1970s onwards. The manufacture of computer technology is currently extremely oil dependent, but it is feasible for carbon-based semiconductor technology to be mostly electrically manufactured.

2. World War III will not break out

Had the hydrocarbon crunch occurred while Communism was still viable, we would have invested our efforts into nuclear fallout shelters and forgone the generation of this document on the assumption that the likely future was obvious. Most fortuitously for human civilisation, today everyone is more or less agreed on some form of Western-style participatory (even if not quite democratic) free market capitalism as the 'correct' economic solution. Much hot air is expended on clashes of civilisations and imminent threats from China/Islam/whatever, and we certainly expect some strategic positioning in the run-up to the hydrocarbon crunch (after all, what do you think the USA in Iraq was all about? Or Russia in Chechnya or Georgia? Or China in Tibet or Africa?). However, today is one of those very few times in human history where everyone is more or less on the same page and moreover, it is extremely, even starkly obvious given the recent economic slide that everyone's fortunes hang upon everyone else's. No one is under any illusions whatsoever that a military grab for resources would do much beyond forestall, and most likely advance, the inevitable.

Much as the powers-that-be might dislike it, we're going to sink or swim together and that creates a wealth of opportunities. In other words, unless a nuclear bomb goes off by accident at a really bad moment (which is quite possible given the age of their control systems), we think that the crunch will be met with military skirmishes around key strategic resource bottlenecks but not full-out war. We expect propaganda from all sides to increase but we anticipate that this will simply drive more people to discover their own truth through the internet – which by the way is extremely hard to comprehensively filter due to its enormous size and diversity. In finding their own truth they shall discover Manifestos for Change of which this, the Neo-Capitalist Manifesto, is to our knowledge the first of the 21st century.

While we would rather prefer that every single proposal in here is enacted exclusive of all others, we know that our proposals will be fused with others and something unexpected to any of us will emerge. It is for this reason that we have attempted to keep the proposals as separate and standalone as we could in the hope that as many of them will be implemented piecemeal as possible.

Nevertheless, it is still possible that Nationalistic fervour may break out in one of the major powers, leading to a belief that the only viable solution is growth through expansion and therefore leading to World War III. We sincerely hope that it does not.

3. There will be a cultural shift towards 'smaller is better'

Most of the proposals made by this Manifesto are plainly infeasible in the current prevailing culture. For example, international and internal treaties technically prohibit much of what we propose – especially within the EU and USA – and no one realistically expects the legal profession to enthusiastically embrace the opening up of Law so that anyone can grasp the general gist from the Parliamentary directives, or the teaching profession the elimination of most of their numbers, or indeed governments themselves who would be relegated to mostly a supervisory role. We recognise that this one argument is the single biggest flaw in our proposals – they may well produce a high growth near-utopia which transcends any civilisation ever witnessed by man, but in the end: *does it matter if it isn't possible?*

We have observed that around the last time oil prices rose substantially in the 1970s there became a most interesting phenomenon: smaller & simpler suddenly became fashionable. This was odd, even at that time, because the average general trend is towards bigger, heavier and more powerful: so for example, after decades of bigger & heavier cars, American consumers suddenly switched their preference towards small Japanese cars much to the then detriment of the Detroit automobile cartel. One might say 'oh that's just because of the rise in petrol prices', but these things become self-reinforcing: smaller stayed better long after the oil price had returned to reasonable levels.

We have noted the recent sudden switch of preference towards smaller, simpler computers: the 10" and 9" laptops and tiny desktop computers of 2008/2009 have been vastly more popular than anyone in the computer industry predicted – even Intel who manufactures the Atom processor which powers most of these 'light' computers was surprised by the massive shift in demand[49]. Last year in Ireland €20k engagement rings were the average, this year any ring over €5k receives a disapproving look and much nastiness in the grapevine gossip. Such is the nature of energy driven recessions – they are one of the few events which have a predictable effect on women's hemlines.

Considering the upcoming hydrocarbon crunch, we believe that this trend towards 'smaller is better' shall go far further this time than at any time in preceding history. Firstly the banks are going to be given a hefty haircut – they were foolish enough to award themselves bonuses out of taxpayers' emergency capital, and they will slowly be savaged for such monumental insensitivity with a thousand cuts. We predict that this will be the first of many 'downsizings' of many of society's big institutions, and much as Thatcher and Reagan were elected in the late 1970s out of society's annoyance with big and incompetent government, we believe that society too will reach the right state of mind to make these proposals viable sooner rather than later. We believe in particular that the time is ripe for massive reform of Education where the death bells for the current system of institutionalised child abuse have been chiming ever louder for decades now – it just needs one large enough crack to let the light shine through, and the entire edifice will collapse.

4. Human Beings will not suddenly start behaving better

Most, if not nearly all, of the existing literature on the topic of mitigating the effects of climate change and/or hydrocarbon scarcity comes from the left wing of politics for the simple reason that it was the left who began the process of telling the world about these upcoming problems (e.g. *Limits to Growth*), and hence it is the left who have done most of the work in thinking of the likely scenarios and solutions. One of the very best series of books in detailing what needs to be done is Lester Brown's excellent *Plan B* books and we strongly encourage anyone interested in this topic to consult them.

---

[49] Intel, being the Intel monopoly, have deliberately gone out of their way to pace this market transition by erecting roadblocks to slow and smooth the adoption of the Atom processor. This is to give the market time to adapt and is probably a wise move despite the consternation of computer enthusiasts who really hate it when a company deliberately denies them new technology.

However, as so often happens, left wing politics got mixed up into the plan for what needs to be done. The left is quite correct that most of our global social and environmental problems stem from two main factors: (i) there are too many people in the world and (ii) too many of those people are extremely poor (i.e. there is a massive and growing wealth gap between the richest and poorest). Having so many extremely poor people is very destructive for the global environment because they are willing to do anything to eke out an existence, and by having so many living on the threshold of subsistence, they tend to wreck their local ecosystems through digging for valuable ores, overfishing, felling trees etc. in the standard Malthusian fashion. The left holds that the only solution is to narrow the wealth gap by reallocating wealth away from the very rich Westerners to the poorest of the world such that all these poor people no longer have to eke out an existence, whereupon the environmental destruction is no longer necessary and the birth rate will normalise. They estimate that the world population could be stabilised via their plan at around nine billion people.

It sounds wonderful doesn't it? The world's peoples coming together to work together as one, the rich giving to the poor and everyone comes out okay. Our problem is that we feel this scenario highly unrealistic because it assumes that *imposing better behaviour makes better people*. The cold, hard truth of our current problem is that most of the world's poorest people exist because their parents had more children than they could provide for – eminently sensible given their experience of the world at that time when most of their children would not reach adulthood. Is it being seriously suggested that if we should transfer wealth from rich Westerners to these poorest of the poor that they will suddenly curtail their birth rate to two children per couple thanks to this global spirit of cooperation in order to mitigate climate change and hydrocarbon crunches?

We think that extremely unlikely. It has been proposed that education programmes accompany the transfer of wealth, but we don't think that most of the poorest people will listen – they will happily take the wealth, but much like first generation immigrants into the West, they will for that first generation act as if they were still much poorer i.e. there is a significant lag between changes in wealth and birth rate. This means that if we transfer that wealth, we must expect a ballooning of population. Of course, the left know this and have tried to account for it using some very optimistic projections. We think these projections are far too optimistic to be realistic, and we worry that should people not follow the optimistic reproduction model, there may become a temptation to introduce a 'food for sterilisation' programme to ensure that people comply. This deeply worries us, because now one set of people are deciding the fate of another set of people without their permission which is the perfect recipe for moral corruption.

Beyond these more fundamental matters, there are also the issues of differences in culture and politics. We would absolutely love if people could put aside their differences and cooperate to solve the world's problems. However, life isn't like that: people compete, and the West above all is very competitive. The average Western consumer is more than happy to see fifteen million people die annually in the third world just because they can't be bothered to spare a dollar each a day – they like their food, electronics and luxuries made cheaper by third world labour eking out a living for pennies. Equally, we are not more generous because we know that for every poor person we save from starvation, currently around four new mouths to feed appear within ten years – the consequence of which is tearing apart Africa and will shortly tear apart India and China. We don't think that the average poor person is going to give a damn about climate change or anything that worries the West because it simply isn't on a person's radar when they regularly fear starvation – though they will get 'worried' if the West pays them to do so, but then that isn't genuine agreement with Western concerns.

Many have said that this is a highly impoverished view of human beings and that we would far prefer to do nothing and let two billion people die a horrific death rather than trying to save them. They therefore say that we are being selfish and that we are abrogating our duty to help our fellow man.

We however believer that we have a wider view. We would point out that we got ourselves into the present position by having dug ourselves into the hole of overpopulation through simultaneously being too miserly to give enough to let the birth rate naturally drop after one generation, and being too charitable to let the starving die thus saving many more deaths later on. In other words, we got to this place through dithering and insecurity: we **must** choose either one way fully or the other way fully. We don't think that anyone on the left or right would disagree with this statement, so now it comes down to which choice will make a better world: save two billion or sacrifice two billion?

We think that nine billion people are far less sustainable than four billion people. They are more unwieldy, harder to control and far more likely to destabilise. They also *de facto* require twice the resources on an ongoing basis. We have also been in this position before: the Scottish Highland Clearances were performed by accountants on the basis that sheep were more profitable than people who couldn't look after themselves and regulate their own birth rate – a similar situation arose in the Irish potato famine. The choices made then by the rich and powerful in the early to mid-19th century transformed the world and contributed very significantly to the rise of the United States of America as the world superpower.

Without doubt, this choice between saving or sacrificing two to three billion people will have just as profound effects in the next two centuries. Which option is more likely to succeed, have more beneficial effects according to the historical record and be long-term sustainable? Choose your poison: We have.

Bibliography

الطـــريق فــي معـالم *(Milestones Along the Way)*. قطـب ســـيد (Sayyid Qutb)

Annila, A. (2011). 'Least-time paths of light'. *Monthly Notices of the Royal Astronomical Society* (doi: 10.1111/j.1365-2966.2011.19242.x).

Arrow, K. (1951). Social Choice and Individual Values. *Cowles Commission for Research in Economics Monographs Series no. 12* .

Arrow, K. (1962). 'The economic implications of Learning by Doing'. *Review of Economic Studies , vo. 29*, pp. 155-173.

Atkinson, Q. D., Meade, A., Venditti, C., Greenhill, S. J., & Pagel, M. (2008, February). 'Languages Evolve in Punctuational Bursts'. *Science , vol. 319* (no. 5863), p. p. 588.

Auffhammer, M., Ramanathan, V., & Vincent, J. R. (2006). 'Integrated model shows that atmospheric brown clouds and greenhouse gases have reduced rice harvests in India'. *Proceedings of the National Academy of Sciences* .

Ayres, R., & Warr, B. (2006). 'Economic growth, technological progress and energy use in the U.S. over the last century: Identifying common trends and structural change in macroeconomic time series'. *INSEAD Working Papers* .

Bakan, J. (2004). *The Corporation: The Pathological Pursuit of Power.* London: Constable & Robinson Ltd.

Bateson, G. (1979). *Mind And Nature - A Necessary Unity.* New York: Dutton.

Bekenstein, J. (2003). 'Information in the Holographic Universe'. *Scientific American , vol. 289* (no. 2), pp. 58-65.

Benton, M., & Twitchett, R. (2003). 'How to kill (almost) all life: the end-Permian extinction event'. *Trends in Ecology & Evolution , vol. 18* (no. 7), pp. 358-365.

Berlin, I. (1979). *Four Essays on Liberty.* Oxford University Press.

Bernstein, W., & Arnott, R. (2003). 'Earnings Growth: The Two Percent Dilution'. *Financial Analysts Journal , vol. 59* (no. 5), pp. 47-55.

Bourdieu, P. (1977). *Outline of a Theory of Practice.* Cambridge University Press.

Bourdieu, P. (1993). *The Field of Cultural Production.* Polity Press.

Bourguignon, F., & Morrisson, C. (2002). 'Inequality among world citizens: 1820-1992'. *American Economic Review , vol. 92* (no. 4), pp. 727-744.

Brooks, F. P. (1975). *The Mythical Man-Month: Essays on Software Engineering.* Addison-Wesley.

Brown, L. (2008). *Plan B 3.0: Mobilizing to Save Civilization.* London: W. W. Norton & Co.

Brutsaert, W., & Parlange, M. B. (1998). 'Hydrologic cycle explains the evaporation paradox'. *Nature , vol. 396* (no. 30).

Capra, F. (1976). *The Tao of Physics.* London: Flamingo.

Capra, F. (1997). *The Web Of Life.* London: Flamingo Books.

Carr, E. H. (1967). *What is History?* London: Penguin Books.

Caves, R. E. (2000). *Creative Industries: Contracts between Art and Commerce.* Harvard University Press.

Cette, G., Kocoglu, Y., & Mairesse, J. (2010). 'Productivity Growth and Levels in France, Japan, the United Kingdom and the United States in the Twentieth Century'. *Banque de France Working Papers .*

Chaitin, G. J. (1990). 'Information, Randomness and Incompleteness'. *World Scientific .*

Cole, H. S., & Pavitt, K. L. (1973). *Models of Doom: A Critique of the Limits to Growth.* Universe Pub.

Costanza, R., d'Arge, R., Groot, R. d., Farber, S., Grasso, M., Hannon, B., et al. (1997). 'The Value of the World's Ecosystem Services and Natural Capital'. *Nature , vol. 387*, pp. 253-260.

Dasgupta, P. (2007). 'Comments on the Stern Review's Economics of Climate Change'. *National Institute Economic Review , no. 199.*

Dasgupta, P. (upcoming). 'Discounting Climate Change'. *Review of Environmental Economics and Policy* .

Datta, S. K., Tauro, A. C., & Balaoing, S. N. (1968). 'Effect of Plant Type and Nitrogen Level on the Growth Characteristics and Grain Yield of Indica Rice in the Tropics'. *Agronomy Journal* .

David, P. A., Waterman, A., & Arora, S. (2003). *'The Free/Libre/Open Source Software Survey for 2003'*. Retrieved from http://www.stanford.edu/group/floss-us/

Debreu, G. (1959). *Theory of Value: An Axiomatic Analysis of Economic Equilibrium.* New Haven: Yale University Press.

Ehrlich, P. R. (1968). *The Population Bomb.* Ballentine Books.

Epple, K., & Schaefer, R. (1996). The transition from monopoly to competition: The case of housing insurance in Baden-Württemberg. *European Economic Review* , *vol. 40*, pp. 1123-1131.

Field, A. (2009). 'US economic growth in the gilded age'. *Journal of Macroeconomics* , *vol. 31* (no. 1), pp. 173-190.

Food and Agriculture Organization. (2003). *World agriculture towards 2015/2030: an FAO perspective.* Rome, Italy.

Fountaine, T. M., Benton, M. J., Dyke, G. J., & Nudds, R. L. (2005). 'The quality of the fossil record of Mesozoic birds'. *Proceedings of the Royal Society in Biological Sciences* , *vol. 272* (no. 1560), pp. 289-294.

Friedman, M., & Friedman, R. (1980). *Free to Choose: A Personal Statement.* New York: Harcourt.

Galbraith, J. K. (1968). *The New Industrial State.* Penguin Books.

Gibbon, E. (1898). *The History of the Decline and Fall of the Roman Empire.* London: Methen & Co.

Gödel, K. (1931). *'On Formally Undecidable Propositions in Principia Mathematica and Related Systems'.*

Gokhale, J. (2009). 'Measuring the Unfunded Obligations of European Countries'. *European Economy Economic Papers* (no. 297).

Graff, D. A., & Higham, R. (2002). *A Military History of China.* Westview Press.

Gramsci, A. (1929-1935). *Prison Notebooks.*

Groningen Growth and Development Centre. (n.d.). *The World Economy: Historical Statistics.* Retrieved from http://www.ggdc.net/

Gruber, N., & Galloway, J. N. (2008). 'An Earth-system perspective of the global nitrogen cycle'. *Nature, vol. 451*, pp. 293-296.

Handy, C. B. (1976). *Understanding Organizations.* London: Penguin Books.

Hatch, M. (2002). 'C4 photosynthesis: discovery and resolution'. *Photosynthesis Research, vol. 73*, pp. 251-256.

Hawkin, P., Lovins, A. B., & Lovins, L. H. (1999). *Natural Capitalism - The Next Industrial Revolution.* London: Earthscan Publications.

Heisenburg, W. (1971). *Der Teil Und Das Ganze (Physics and Beyond).* New York: Harper & Row.

Hesmondhalgh, D. (2006). 'Bourdieu, the media and cultural production'. *Media, Culture and Society, vol. 28*, pp. 211-231.

Hewlett, S., & Luce, C. (2006). 'Extreme jobs - the dangerous Allure of the 70-hour workweek'. *Harvard Business Review, vol. 84* (no. 12), pp. 49-59.

Hofstadter, D. R. (1979). *Gödel Escher Bach – An Eternal Golden Braid.* London: Harvester Press.

Homer-Dixon, T. (2007). *The Upside of Down.* London: Souvenir Press.

Hotelling, H. (1929). 'Stability in Competition'. *The Economic Journal, vol. 39*, pp. 41-57.

Hubbert, M. K. (1956). 'Nuclear Energy and the Fossil Fuels'. *American Petroleum Institute.*

International Cooperative Alliance . (2007). *Annual Report.*

International Monetary Fund. (2008). *World Economic Outlook Database.*

International Rice Research Institute. (2008). *The Decline of IR8.* Retrieved from http://www.irri.org/publications/annual/pdfs/ar2000/IR8.pdf

IPCC. (2007). *The Fourth Assessment Report.* United Nations.

Jackson, N., & Carter, P. (2006). *Rethinking Organisational Behaviour: A Poststructuralist Framework.* London: Prentice Hall.

Jantsch, E. (1980). *The Self-Organizing Universe.* New York: Pergamon.

Jevons, W. S. (1865). *The Coal Question; an inquiry concerning the progress of the nation, and the probable exhaustion of our Coal-Mines.* London: Macmillan.

Johansson, C., Norman, M., & Gidhagen, L. (2007). 'Spatial & temporal variations of PM10 and particle number concentrations in urban air'. *Environmental Monitoring and Assessment , vol. 127* (no. 1-3), pp. 477-487.

Jorgenson, D. W., & Vu, K. (2005). 'Information Technology and the World Economy'. *Scandinavian Journal of Economics , vol. 107* (no. 4), pp. 631-650.

Jung, C. G. (1964). *Man and his Symbols.* New York: Anchor Books, Doubleday.

Kaye, P., Laflamme, R., & Mosca, M. (2006). *Introduction to Quantum Computing.* London: Oxford University Press.

Kittel, C., & Kroemer, H. (1980). *Thermal Physics.* W.H. Freeman & Co Ltd.

Kuhn, T. S. (1962). *The Structure of Scientific Revolutions.* University of Chicago Press.

Layard, R. (2006). *Happiness: Lessons from a New Science.* Penguin Books.

Liepert, B. G. (2002). 'Observed Reductions in Surface Solar Radiation in the United States and Worldwide from 1961 to 1990'. *Geophysical Research Letters , vol. 29* (no. 12), pp. 1421.

Liu, Z., & Spiegel, M. (2011). 'Boomer retirement: headwinds for US equity markets'. *FRBSF Economic Letter .*

Lovelock, J. (2007). *The Revenge of Gaia: Why the Earth Is Fighting Back - and How We Can Still Save Humanity.* Penguin Books Ltd.

Mallory, W. H. (1926). *China: Land of Famine.* American Geographical Society.

Malthus, T. (1798). *An Essay on the Principle of Population.*

Mas-Colell, A., Whinston, M., & Green, J. R. (1995). *Microeconomic Theory.* New York: Oxford University Press.

Maturana, H., & Varela, F. (1987). *The Tree of Knowledge - Knowing That We Know.* Boston: Shambhala.

Meadows, D., Randers, J., & Meadows, D. (2004). *Limits to Growth: The 30-Year Update.* Chelsea Green.

Mikkonen, T., Vadén, T., & Vainio, N. (2007). *'The Protestant ethic strikes back: Open source developers and the ethic of Capitalism'.* Retrieved from http://www.firstmonday.org/issues/issue12_2/mikkonen/index.html

Miller, G. (1971). *Energetics, Kinetics and Life.* Wadsworth.

Newbury, D., & Stiglitz, J. (1982). The Choice of Techniques and the Optimality of Market Equilibrium with Rational Expectations. *Journal of Political Economy , vol. 90* (no. 2), pp. 223-246.

Nordhaus, W. D. (2007). 'A Review of the Stern Review on the Economics of Climate Change'. *Journal of Economic Literature , vol. 45* (3), pp. 686-702.

O' Brien, P., & Clesse, A. (2002). *Two Hegemonies: Britain 1846-1914 and the United States 1941-2001.* Ashgate.

Ormerod, P. (1998). *Butterfly Economics.* London: Faber and Faber Ltd.

Ormerod, P. (2005). *Why Most Things Fail – Evolution, Extinction & Economics.* London: Faber and Faber Ltd.

Osbourne, C. P., & Beerling, D. J. (2006). 'Nature's green revolution: the remarkable evolutionary rise of C4 plants'. *Philosophical Transactions of the Royal Society , vol. 361*, pp. 173-194.

OTA, K.-i. (2006). *Towards a Hydrogen Economy.* Retrieved from OECD Global Science Forum: http://www.oecd.org/dataoecd/12/53/36746578.pdf

Pagel, M., Venditti, C., & Meade, A. (2006, October). 'Large Punctuational Contribution of Speciation to Evolutionary Divergence at the Molecular Level'. *Science , vol. 314* (no. 5796), pp. pp. 119 - 121.

Penrose, R. (2004). *The Road to Reality.* Great Britain: Random House.

Petit, J. R., Jouzel, J., Raynaud, D., Barkov, N. I., Barnola, J.-M., Basile, I., et al. (1999). 'Climate and atmospheric history of the past 420,000 years from the Vostok ice core, Antarctica'. *Nature*, vol. *399*, pp. 429-436.

Pidwirny, M. (2006). *Fundamentals of Physical Geography, 2nd Edition.* Retrieved from "The Hydrologic Cycle": http://www.physicalgeography.net/fundamentals/8b.html

Porter, M. E. (1980). *Competitive Strategy: Techniques for Analyzing Industries and Competitors.* New York: The Free Press.

Portmann, F., Siebert, S., & Döll, P. (2006). Global dataset of monthly crop-specific irrigated areas around the year 2000. *Conference on International Agricultural Research for Development.* Bonn.

Priest, G. (1979). 'The logic of paradox'. *Journal of Philosophical Logic*, vol. *8*, pp. 219-41.

Ramanathan, V., & Carmichael, G. (2008). 'Global and regional climate changes due to black carbon'. *Nature Geoscience*, vol. *1*, pp. 221-227.

Redefining Progress. (2008). *Genuine Progress Indicator.* Retrieved from http://www.rprogress.org/sustainability_indicators/genuine_progress_i ndicator.htm

Rockström, J. (2003). 'Water for Food and Nature in Drought-Prone Tropics: Vapour Shift in Rain-Fed Agriculture'. *Philosophical Transactions: Biological Sciences*, vol. *358* (no. 1440), pp. 1997-2009.

Rosegrant, M., Cai, X., & Cline, S. (2002). *World water and food to 2025: dealing with scarcity.* Washington D.C.: International Food Policy Research Institute.

Runge, C. F., & Senauer, B. (2007). *'How Biofuels Could Starve the Poor'.* Retrieved from Foreign Affairs: http://www.foreignaffairs.org/20070501faessay86305/c-ford-runge-benjamin-senauer/how-biofuels-could-starve-the-poor.html?mode=print

Russell, B. (1946). *A History of Western Philosophy.* London: George Allen & Unwin Ltd.

Ryle, G. J., Powell, C. E., & Gordon, A. J. (1979). 'The Respiratory Costs of Nitrogen Fixation in Soyabean, Cowpea, and White Clover'. *Journal of Experimental Botany*, vol. *30* (no. 1), pp. 145-153.

Shady, R., Haas, J., & Creamer, W. (2001). Dating Caral, a Preceramic Site in the Supe Valley on the Central Coast of Peru. *Science , vo. 292*, pp. pp. 723-726.

Shapiro, C., & Varian, H. R. (1998). *Information Rules: A Strategic Guide to the Network Economy.* Harvard Business School Press.

Sharpe, W. F. (1964). Capital asset prices: A theory of market equilibrium under conditions of risk. *Journal of Finance , vol. 19* (no. 3), pp. 425-442.

Simon, J. L. (1994). 'More People, Greater Wealth, More Resources, Healthier Environment'. *Journal of Economic Affairs .*

Simon, J. L. (1981). *The Ultimate Resource.* Princeton University Press.

Smil, V. (2001). *Enriching the Earth: Fritz Haber, Carl Bosch and the Transformation of World Food Production.* Cambridge, MA: MIT Press.

Smuts, J. (1926). *Holism and Evolution.* London: Penguin Books.

Stern, N. (2007). *The Economics of Climate Change: The Stern Review.* Cambridge University Press.

Stewart, I. (1997). *Does God Play Dice? - The New Mathematics of Chaos.* Penguin Books.

Taiz, L., & Zeiger, E. (2006). *Plant Physiology 4th ed.* Sinauer Associates, Inc.

Takáts, E. (2010). 'Ageing and asset prices'. *BIS Working Papers .*

The Cooperative Group. (2006). *Annual General Report.* Manchester: The Cooperative Group.

The International Co-operative Alliance. (2006). *Annual Report 2006.* Geneva: International Co-operative Alliance.

The World Bank. (2006). *Water, Electricity, and the Poor.*

Tol, R. (2006). 'The Stern Review of the economics of climate change: a comment'. *Energy & Environment , vol. 17* (no. 6), pp. 977-981.

U.S. Department of Agriculture and Agricultural Research Service. (2006). *History of the Green Revolution.* Retrieved from http://www.ars.usda.gov/is/timeline/green.htm

U.S. Department of Agriculture and Agricultural Research Service. (2006).
    'Improving Corn'. Retrieved from
    http://www.ars.usda.gov/is/timeline/corn.htm

US Census Bureau. (2008). Retrieved from
    http://www.census.gov/ipc/www/idb/worldpopinfo.html

Verhulst, P. F. (1838). 'Notice sur la loi que la population poursuit dans son
    accroissement'. *Correspondance mathématique et physique*, vol. 10,
    pp. 113-121.

Walsch, N. D. (1997). *Conversations with God: An Uncommon Dialogue: Book
    1*. G. P. Putnam & Sons.

Watson, A. M. (1974). 'The Arab Agricultural Revolution and Its Diffusion,
    700-1100'. *The Journal of Economic History*, vol. 34 (no. 1), pp. 8-35.

White, S., & Cordell, D. (2009). 'Peak Phosphorus: the sequel to Peak Oil'.
    Global Phosphorus Research Initiative .

Whitehead, A. N., & Russell, B. (1911-1913). *Principia Mathematica (3 vols)*.
    Cambridge University Press.

Wild, M., Gilgen, H., Roesch, A., Ohmura, A., Long, C. N., Dutton, E. G., et al.
    (2005). 'From Dimming to Brightening: Decadal Changes in Solar
    Radiation at Earth's Surface'. *Science*, vol. 308 (no. 5723), pp. 847-
    850.

Wilkinson, W. (2007). 'In Pursuit of Happiness Research: Is It Reliable? What
    Does It Imply for Policy?'. *Policy Analysis* (no. 590).

World Health Organisation. (2002). *World Health Report*.

World Resources Institute. (2007). *'Agricultural Production Indices: Food
    Production per Capita Index'*. Retrieved from EarthTrends:
    http://earthtrends.wri.org/

Xie, J. et al. (2011). 'Social Consensus through the influence of committed
    minorities'. *Phys. Rev. E*, vol. 84 (no. 1), id. 10.1103.

Zeitlyn, D. (2003). 'Gift economies in the development of open source software:
    anthropological reflections'. *Research Policy*, vol. 32 (no. 7), pp.
    1287-1291.